Off-Beat Spark

Quirky **light & dark poems** for life's ups & downs

David Hardy

EMPIRE
PUBLICATIONS

First published in 2023

EMPIRE PUBLICATIONS
1 Newton Street, Manchester M1 1HW
© David Hardy 2023

ISBN: 978-1-915616-09-8

CONTENTS

Acknowledgements

Special thanks to Mick Middles without whom this book would not exist. I would also like to thank Andrew James Galloway for his constructive criticism and Valerie Bell for her encouragement and support

Dedication

Dedicated to Paul Hillyard. Gone but not forgotten

About the Poet

David Hardy's early literary endeavours comprised writing poems for friends and recording daily happenings and flights of the imagination. Covering a broad range of subjects, his work is infused with humour and pathos, light and dark.

An occasional contributor to the American Music Magazine, *Rock at Night*, David is currently building up a following on the open mic circuit in Greater Manchester. He lives in Marple, Cheshire, and he enjoys both community activities and 'soaking up' the solitude in the Peak District

Foreword

The first time ever I saw David Hardy's face... well, he was striding gleefully toward me across a petrol station forecourt in Stockport. This was amid the kaleidoscopic era of the early to mid-1980s. I don't know if we were fully aware of the cultural bounties we were wading through at the time, but it certainly helped us to build a friendship that managed to survive the second half of the decade when we didn't see each other. Back then and, in an instant, we were zipping through the dank pubs of that northern town while feverishly dissecting myriad musics, films, books, plays, TV chat shows...anything really. It was almost as if we actually sensed that there might come a time when we would find ourselves dumped in some barren tundra where little aesthetic endeavour would be allowed to thrive.

Dave certainly knew his stuff, from the doom-laden Johns of Martyn and Cale to lighter fare from the fringes of the lively charts.

Back then I was acquainted with a good many music writers, and while I enjoyed their company I felt they laboured under the restraints of suffocating egos. Dave was free of such shackles. His enthusiasm seemed to flow with an uncomplicated ease. It was, and remains, a pleasure to chat with him even if the music and art seem rather distant, a little like our current pubs of choice which are mostly away from teaming Manctopia and tastefully lurking in some rural idyll.

One thing I always sensed was, to steal an ancient adage, he was always a poet. Always. But it was there, lurking mischievously within his private shadows.

I was, therefore, delighted and not a bit surprised when the dam finally burst and his torrent of words flooded the welcoming valley. Well, Facebook anyway and, again, how wonderful to see his words invading that unholy assemblage of bitterness and narcissistic spite. It's never like that with

Dave. His vivid sideways glances at an absurd world have arrived daily…often more frequently than that, but they are always welcome, always illuminating and blessed with… well, something else. Dave's poetry flies between the black and the white, the tastefully mundane and the disturbingly honest, gloriously light and feverishly introspective. That's the bomb, right there. Up and down, outlandish and reclusive. But forever honest. Forever true.

Above all, what a joy to see them gathering so deservedly here. What a joy! What a joy!

Mick Middles
September 2023

A Kestrel for a Knave

I

Kes Ascends

A cold and chilly morning
In Barnsley or a similar place
An undernourished bird of prey
Brings a smile to a tortured face

All of life's disappointments
Are suddenly cast aside
A kestrel, a friend, a confidante
In whom he can confide

Flying high, almost balletic
In the slipstream of all dreams
Hovering above, conveying love
Oblivious to earthly themes

Silent overhead swirling
Bewitching acrobatic spree
A flute interrupting the silence
The sound of 'Kes Flying Free'

Tremulous, mesmerising
Delivered with the utmost care
The flute is a magical instrument
In the hands of Harold McNair

Surveying the earth below
Squawking, a familiar cry
Image of unshackled beauty
Mirrored in tamer's eye

Gentleness and jesses
A descent to tamer's hand
Collision of boy and kestrel
Brief containment and command

Jesses mean in Hebrew
That God (really) exists
In moments of such wonder
Nagging doubts no longer persist

II

Billy Casper

Tormented working-class boy
Abused at school and home
Lying low during lessons
Allowing his mind to roam

A harsh life for Billy
Dragged up by a single mother
Facing a bleak existence
With a bastard for a brother

On the wrong side of authority
In a brutal educational regime
Headmaster wielding the cane
Venting of his spleen

Shouting and humiliation
'Casper, get on your feet!'
'You weren't paying attention, Casper!'
'Casper, you were half asleep!'

'Yes Sir, no Sir'
Reducing a lad to tears
Corporal punishment at its worst
Preying on deep-rooted fears

Mr Sugden, the sports teacher
He doesn't understand

Mr Farthing tries his best
With sympathy on demand

Billy speaks to the Careers Adviser
But the options are truly shit
'There's nowt round here to do'
'Cos I'm not going down the pit'

Finding a kestrel on a farm
Changed a young boy's life
Provided temporary respite
From endless pain and strife

III

Kes Dies

Jud is a bastard
Let's have this said upfront
A completely immoral person
Not someone to confront

He spends all his time
When he's not down the pit
Raising his hands in anger
He doesn't give a shit

A stern rebuke for Billy
When he fails to place Jud's bet
A day he'll remember forever
A day of sorrow and regret

Kes thrown in the dustbin
Billy lashes out at Jud
'Why did you have to kill Kes?'
'Destroying all that's good'

Final resting place
Is a ramshackle grave
No longer occupying the skies
A kestrel for a knave

David Hardy

"They beat him
They deprived him
They ridiculed him
They broke his very *heart*
But they couldn't break his spirit"

Till death, Kes, we do part

A Kestrel for a Knave is the name of a book by Barry Hines, and the last verse in italics is taken from a publicity poster for the screen adaptation, *Kes*.

14

ABSTRACT

I've always appreciated abstraction. It seems to be a major part of my psyche. From the depths of my mind they arise, these strange, unfettered connections, moving here, moving there, moving in different directions. Yes, I guess we all possess a certain amount of weirdness, don't we?

Losang Dragpa

Architect of all dreams
Hold this vision in your hand
Lay foundations that will last
No more castles in the sand

Builder of all rainbows
When sunshine follows rain
Bathe me in your healing
Protect me from all pain

Creator of all consciousness
Keep me safely in your care
Shower me with your wisdom
Help free me from despair

Constructor of all compassion
Cradle my innocence in your heart
Now safeguarded in your divinity
Never shall we part

Dreaming

I was breathing underwater
Improbable as it seems
Limbs outstretched like a starfish
Immersed in nautical themes

Transfixed by everything before me
In my wondrous underwater garden
Released from humdrum reality
Granted an aquatic pardon

Suddenly I awoke from my slumber
Returned to being a drowning man
Dogged by the consequences
Of a limited lifespan

I'll go swimming again
Moving along the ocean bed
Unconsciously processing everything
I ever did or said

Meet you on the cusp
On the very edge of meaning
Where thoughts are gently healed
Through the mystery of dreaming

David Hardy

Bad Dreams

Entropic, captive and unconscious
Dark menacing themes
Taken hostage in your slumber
Crushed in a world of dreams

Years of painful experience
Worked through during the day
Only to be relived at night-time
As demons come out to play

Some journeys seem unbearable
Mantraps and foreboding strangers
You're moving in slow motion
Navigating endless dangers

A fire below is burning
Rats abandoning ship
On the edge of a plank you stand
Enduring an excruciating trip

You take the deepest of breaths
Before confronting the perilous sea
Suddenly you awaken
In that moment you are free

Watching The World Go By

He was wearing a Wet Leg t-shirt
To celebrate his eighty-third
It was just another day
In the theatre of the absurd

Mounted his mobility scooter
A big smile on his face
Veering to the left, right and centre
In a vehicle disability race

A woman with a baby
At the opposite side of the bench
I really should make a move
But moving is such a wrench

Everyday observations
In a busy shopping mall
An antidote to excitement
But who knows, who can tell?

I'm waiting in anticipation
To find out what will happen next
No doubt I'll communicate any updates
With a series of misguided texts

Drug Dealer

Drug dealer, drug dealer
Don't come on to me
'No thanks' to your illicit substances
And samples given for free

Twiddling with your roll-up
Inhaling fumes is tragic
I'd rather a full English
Though I believe your mushrooms are magic

You spoke of the ancient shaman
And past life regressions
The spiritual path you follow
Now free from all possessions

You then went off at a tangent
Told me of your potions
A mind-bending cocktail
For soothing my emotions

Peering through your dreadlocks
Wearing a pork pie hat
Talking about conspiracies
Whilst fumbling with your cravat

You mentioned the sacred plants
Mother Earth and Father Sun
That one day we'll all be unified
When the Spirit's work is done

But what really swung it
What filled me with the utmost mirth
Was your firmly held belief
That aliens inhabited the Earth

So, I'll bid you farewell
I hope that you'll be fine
You'll have to find another
With whom to commit a crime

Drug dealer, drug dealer
I'm speaking earnestly
I'm rejecting your instant karma
Please stay away from me

Career Options

Could have been a politician
Something of a chancer
Constitutionally incapable
Of a 'yes' or 'no' answer

Possibly a CEO
A mover and a shaker
A day of reckoning looming
Soon to meet my maker

Perhaps an investment banker
Not a penny left to share
Indifferent to the plight of others
In a world where I don't care

A major shareholder
Of a multinational corporation
Overcome with joy
At financial deregulation

What about a preacher?
Offering evangelical interventions
Freeing us all from sin
Driven by God intentions

A green grocer, a sous chef
How about a candlestick maker?
Let me be anything at all
Other than a hapless faker

Enter Centre Stage

Enter centre stage
You carefully learned your lines
A pitch-perfect performance
Every single time

The crowds and your contemporaries
Admired your acting skill
One moment you were disarming
In another your looks could kill

But no one can go on indefinitely
Those adverse reviews you feared
Came from the critics who adored you
Tastes changing down the years

Exit centre stage
The show will go on
They'll be other dramatic entrances
Even though your time is done

Time that you were going
Slowly drifting away
You used to rehearse your words
Now you've nothing left to say

Contradictions

Circuit breakers and curtain raisers
Fine lines between friendship and foe
Never knowing if red is for adventure
Or whether green means that you should go

Contradictions and coincidences
Stopping short or revealing all
Running away towards yourself
Tripping up after a fall

Parallels and cul-de-sacs
Other routes navigated with care
Haphazard journeys in the dark
Would-be destinations – of ecstasy and despair

Spineless

Emotionally thwarted
Hard shell corrugation
Exo-skeleton meltdown
Crustacean depreciation

Time to re-invent
Tentacled distraction
Soft anemones abound
Much to my satisfaction

Thin skinned aspiration
A viewpoint to opine
With, without or otherwise
Skeletal decline

Perhaps now is the time
For rest and recreation
Floating along the seabed
Embracing oscillation

Smooching along the sand
An entirely jellified creature
Boneless and bona fide
Exceptional underwater feature

Random Conversations

It's all changed, it's not the same
What do you know? Blah de blah
Taxi to The Sycamore in ten minutes
Probably not that far

Tell him to suck it up
Nothing less than he deserves
To use a footballing analogy
Stick him in the reserves

There's a picture of me on Facebook
With Tamsin, Amy and Kirsty
Do mum and dad know
'Bout the court appearance on Thursday?

Henry! Jesus, what's he doing?
Can't you keep your dog at bay?
Doesn't it bother you at all
What other people might say?

Why wouldn't you get the loan?
Fifteen minutes, if you go on line
Your credit rating's good
Everything will be fine

I've always been a snacker
I'm a binge eater for sure
I've got to keep on eating
Till I can't take any more

The folks are at it again
Dad's just written a will
His sister's a beneficiary
If only looks could kill

Have you finished eating?
Was everything okay?
An out-of-town pub
On a conversive sunny day

Every Occasion

There's a poem for every occasion
A trivial or momentous event
From the affection of a loving mother
To adhering to the rigours of Lent

From a few derisory words
That flow contemptuously from your lips
To the aftermath of a war
Or an impending apocalypse

A birth, a wedding, a funeral
Joyfulness begetting sorrow
A pyre floating down a river
With no thought of tomorrow

Religious and pagan celebrations
The solemnity of Christian traditions
Dancing jovially around a maypole
Adopting different positions

Shattered dreams that really mattered
Earthbound or heaven-sent
Sat here in contemplation
Awaiting another event

Words and Colours

If only I could paint in words
Where pigments and writings are bled
Expand my colourfield vocabulary
Beyond the confines of A to Z

You could visit my public gallery
Where seascapes and languages emerge
Where limitations no longer exist
And painting and words converge

Watercolours, oils, and acrylics
A canvas of intonations
Speaking in foreign dialects
So many derivations

I smile at my unworldliness
To explain, I need more prep
But every journey I am told
Begins with the very first step

A flurry of magpie feathers
The onset of an incantation
Noise of an oncoming walker
Breaks my concentration

Black, Red, Green and Blue

The infinite universe above
With stars you can almost feel
The attire at a funeral procession
Or a Henry Ford automobile
Tarmac smouldering on the highway
Rhymes with Jack Kerouac
He's on the road again
And never will come back

The Devil in Dante's Inferno
A cut that almost bled
A hot poker that was brandished
Friendship hanging by a thread
Memories of the fallen
Messages written in blood
Poppies blowing in the wind
We fondly remember the good

Naivety of the unworldly
Such foolishness exists
In a world of vested interests
Old jealousies persist
Apples from the grocery store
A householder mows his grass
Tepid conversation with a neighbour
Soon will surely pass

The deepest of all the oceans
And the sky looming overhead
A mood of prevailing sadness
The mourning of the dead
Forget-me-nots in the fields
The commitment of the few
A condition of utmost loyalty
A new order that is true

Eclectic Ladyland

Troublesome thoughts are everywhere
In this synaptic constellation
Unsanitary, unmade and unholy
Like a Tracey Emin installation

King Crimson clock is ticking
In a progressive kind of way
Thoughts are settling down now
Exposed to the light of day

Second cup of coffee
And the fogginess disappears
Cuckooland by Robert Wyatt
Is music to my ears

I'll hit the gym this morning
Or I'll climb that nearby hill
A musical group once remarked
Can't buy a thrill

Art, music and literature
Simple pleasures in life today
Give me a few moments longer
And I'll be on my Hemingway

Creative Impasse

Paragon of high viscosity
Trapped, muddled and mired
Wading through the treacle
Waiting to be inspired

Sometimes ideas unfurl
As ferns growing wild
Petrified like a forest
Or a small and frightened child

Love, death and humour
Are always popular themes
Conjuring up ideas
From the depths of hidden dreams

Liquidation may be the answer
Creativity's gone awry
What use is pen and paper?
If the words no longer fly

Surely a temporary hiatus
Writers block galore
Sleep well tonight, my friend
Tomorrow, write some more

DEATH

Death is a difficult subject to broach, and for me it has so many different dimensions; from the sheer horror of young lives being taken away ('No More') and the sad loss of a dear friend ('A Poem for Paul') to the inevitable ending of all our lives and what this might mean ('Stardust').

No More

Two sets of parents are weeping
Over their two children – dead
I never caught the news
Just overheard what other people said

Football fans I'm told
Faithful to Man United FC
Future no longer to look forward to
No dreams to set them free

Of cheering their soccer heroes
Watching Red Devils marching to glory
End of youthful exuberance
Final chapter in a very short story

All now is gone
No more – the only words left
Except for the tears of the grieving
Hearts torn, helpless and bereft

No more mornings to start each day with
Rushing to get to school
No more fooling around on the bus
Fancying the boy who's trying to be cool

No more opportunities to grow
Through a spirited adolescent phase
No more birthdays, or celebrations
Never to be twenty-one – no glasses to be raised

No more joy, no pain, no suffering
In discovering who you are
No more fashions, make-up, and mistakes
Passing your exams, or driving your first car

No more chances to find that special someone
To love with all your heart
No more vows for you to make
Like till death do us part

No more ageing and finding wisdom
Happy memories or recounting sorrows
No more of anything
And no more brave tomorrows

Stardust

Weightless, floating upwards
With effortless grace and poise
Light years away from home
Uprooted from earthly noise

Silent, still and hovering
Defying gravitational pull
Overwhelmed by infinite space
Senses working to the full

No need to breathe anymore
Immune to zero atmosphere
Transfixed by the star-filled heavens
Welcoming the end of fear

Unimaginable beauty surrounds you
Body no longer exists
You're everything and nothing
Eternity stands in your midst

This is the future ahead of you
When all has been done and said
A spirit floating freely
Circling silently overhead

Seaside Tragedy

He was standing on the esplanade
When the waves came crashing in
The rip-roaring tide
And your patience wearing thin

You remember shouting out to him
On that sad and fateful day
As he fell from the retaining wall
And was tragically swept away

Flowers were tied to the railings
A tribute and memorial of sorts
A crushing reminder of your child
Constantly in your thoughts

Extinguished by nature's ferocity
By a freak and unexpected wave
His body was never found
Cold and dark deep-sea grave

Anger and helplessness prevail
Underpinned by endless despair
Clenching your fists together
How could life be so unfair?

A Poem for Paul

The raising of an eyebrow
The welcoming smile
Prelude to a conversation
That will engage and beguile

I always had a feeling
That you knew more than you said
The joy for me of unravelling
An encyclopaedic thread

It wasn't just your love of music
A passion that we shared
It was through a connection of like minds
That a friendship was declared

Dearly, dearly missed
Your passing does not make sense
I struggle to find the words
That offer any recompense

On reflection, I hold my hand up
Because it's so plain to see
The legacy that you left
For friends and family

And so it's getting late
Endless thoughts pass through
So many people you loved
I'll take my place in the queue

Irreversible Cessation of Functions

Inevitable sadness for some
Rejoicing in certain quarters
Reactions vary considerably
From detractors and supporters

Does it matter how you were remembered?
On this, I'm not so sure
Disregarded opinions
To gain a few years more

An extension wasn't forthcoming
Sadly you were outvoted
Death came with a vengeance
It wasn't sugar coated

Where did you go to my friend?
When the mist finally descended
A spiritual dimension or nothingness?
On your world view it depended

Onslaught is complete
The point of saturation
No stumbling further forward
End of this narration

Excerpt from a Funeral

Oblivion
That's where I want to be
There's nothing worth holding onto
No illusion of being free

Come on now my friend
Embrace an honoured stance
Death is inevitable
For fuck's sake have a dance

You could have been something
Exceptionally more
I won't forget the life you lived
And no one is keeping score

HUMOUR

Having a sense of humour was something which helped me to
survive the rigours of being a pupil at a second-rate secondary
school. Certainly, it was a great mechanism for disarming
bullies and charming teachers, although it didn't improve my
grades. Digging deeper, I need to thank my mum for my sense
of humour. She was a very funny lady. Bless her.

Hypochondria

I hope I'm not a hypochondriac
Let me wholeheartedly share
That I recently uprooted a follicle
It's alopecia, I do swear

Pricked my thumb with a needle
There was no coagulation
Perhaps quarantine is the answer
Of indeterminable duration

A case of garlic breath
Possibly halitosis
Minor alcohol consumption
The onset of cirrhosis?

Time for a body transplant
Internal organs first
Outer limbs can follow
As I know I have been cursed

With ailments that are real
No longer in my mind
I'm sure my short sightedness
Is a precursor to going blind

Fly

I should not have killed you
You weren't doing any harm
Your proboscis and compound eyes
Hold a certain kind of charm

I suppose I'm a bit sentimental
Should the truth be really known
Brought you down with a tea towel
Your final flight now flown

But let's get this in perspective
Time for a reality check
Before I'm consumed with guilt
As you meander towards the deck

I was brought up to despise you
In this world you should not fit
Occupying my home
After treading in, and eating shit

Waving the tea towel aloft
All of a sudden, I start to cry
'Die, die, you little bastard'
'You dirty bloody fly'

Hotel Booking

I was planning to attend an event
Towards the end of May
Approached a nearby hostelry
With details of my stay

The Sales Manager of the hotel
Quickly confirmed the cost
For a moment I was speechless
For words I was lost

'For two nights, you must be joking'
I proceeded to state my case
'I'm sure the people in Oldham are friendly
And that it's a lovely place'

'But it's not the centre of the universe
It's hardly Lake Garda
To justify these prices
You're going to have to try harder'

Our conversation continued
I imagined her face was like thunder
She stood her ground with conviction
As if Chadderton is the world's seventh wonder

And so I crumbled
At the conclusion of our debate
A couple of expensive nights in Oldham
Kinda seems to be my fate

Had Another Drink

An explosion of activity
Laughing, dancing, singing
Hands joined in unity
Populous really swinging

A time for fun and games
Not to be seriously invested
Give me some open space
The high street is becoming congested

Camaraderie in buckets
The boys are back in town
I'm trying to slot in neatly
Another pint goes down

Talking to somebody or other
In a blur of my own making
Suddenly I'm in a round
Over-consumption is overtaking

So I bought him a beer
Whoever he might have been
An upstanding member of the community
Before flexing the alcohol gene

Decided to head for home
Needed some time to think
Raised my glass to all and sundry
And finished my final drink

Fragmented Thoughts

I watched a music festival
On Netflix the other day
Skinny naked people
Coming out to play

Almost pre-dated McDonald's
Now obesity is everywhere
Deliveroo, Click and Collect
Too lazy to leave the chair

Don't get me on my soapbox
Marc Bolan is doing a session
Netflix enthusiasm waning
It's a gentle kind of regression

Revisiting the Seventies
What a decade that proved to be
Shedloads of exuberance
Flashes of integrity

I'm still distracted by Netflix
White Rabbit by Grace Slick
Reference readily understood
By music writer, Mick

So here's the point in summary
The hippies had it good
Netflix is shit, I am distracted
I hope that's understood

Dinosaur

Time for me to move on
I'm sure you get the gist
I hope your fossilised remains
Are bequeathed to a palaeontologist

Dead as a dodo you are
Certainly from the neck above
A relic by all accounts
An exponent of cupboard love

I'm turning a page in a book
Starting a new chapter
Emotionally you're a dinosaur
A small-brained velociraptor

I meant to mention it before
But I didn't have the chops
Perhaps you're a larger creature
A vegetable-eating triceratops

Any which way you look at it
You're a person of distinction
You definitely belong in a museum
Still awaiting your timely extinction

Dental Floss

Without dental floss
Where would we be?
Mint flavoured unwaxed
Is the one for me

A valuable activity
To which I attest
Arrest gingivitis
A condition I detest

Work it up and down
Forward and back
With decisive motions
To remove that plaque

Floss is underrated
And it's such a relief
A simple routine
To save my teeth

Creative Criminality

Judge, jury and executioner
Determining my creative crimes
I'm guilty on all counts, my Lord
Of writing poems that rhyme

Frowned on in certain circles
At least that's what I suppose
I wonder how long the sentence is
For shamefully abandoning prose

With a certain number of syllables
And a tried and trusted metre
I rest my case completely
My defence could not be sweeter

All this free-flowing stuff
Give me a sonnet anytime
A clearly defined structure
That is rhythmically aligned

So I don't know much about writing
But I do know how to shock
My ignorance won't save me this time
As they lead me from the dock

Cooking for a King

Henry the Eighth was prolific
He had many a mid-life crisis
He seduced women into wedlock
With his herbs, and his spices

Catherine of Tarragon he divorced
He preferred sweets to savoury
She wasn't much cop in the kitchen
A victim of culinary slavery

Anne Boleyn was not so fortunate
Beheaded for high treasoning
In the corianders of power
Condemned for lack of seasoning

The thyme came for Jane Seymour
She curried flavour with the King
Died after giving birth
Spicy food was not her thing

Anne of Cloves was divorced
Garlic breath her calling card
Keeping Henry at a distance
Was really not that hard

Another head on the chopping block
Parsley, rosemary and sage
Catherine Howard met her maker
Before takeaways were all the rage

The final wife survived
Fenneled her emotions into hatred
Catherine Parr was her name
And her cookbook was overrated

If you're not into herbs and spices
If it's just not your thing
Try to keep your head on
When cooking for a king

Cat's Life

You are so very lucky
To have a carer like no other
A playmate and a friend
Above all, a surrogate mother

A hand glides across your tummy
Your curiosity is always satisfied
As winter nights draw nearer
With whom do you reside?

For you every day is Christmas
Three Kings bearing gold, frankincense, and myrrh
I'd be in Heaven in your position
Apparently, you just purr

I'm not saying that I am jealous
And you're not an object for me to eschew
Sure it's a cat's life all right
What I wouldn't give to be you

David Hardy

Bus Journey

It wasn't a distant journey, admittedly
But I thought I'd catch the bus
I was thinking about *Tom and Jerry*
And a cartoon called 'Heavenly Puss'

Anyway, this transport collective
Was peppered with 'Stepford Wives'
The indomitable living dead
Passengers in their own lives

They were transfixed by mobile phones
Looking miserable as hell
I was awaiting the end of my journey
To be saved by the bell

And whilst I wasn't expecting elation
It was such a pleasant surprise
When the gobby youths left early
Before I instigated their demise

I'll travel on this single-decker again
But not mid-week at 3.30
When the teenagers have just left school
And the regulars are somewhat shirty

British Comedy Films

The good, the bad, the ukulele
Let's leave the ugly there
George Formby cleaning windows
Smiling without a care

Wisdom, the Norman conquest
The film *A Stitch in Time*
'Mr Grimsdale!' hollered Pitkin
Comedy actor in his prime

Game, set and match
Stroking his moustache
'Hard cheese, old boy'
Terry Thomas made a dash

To his sports car and doting girlfriend
Leaving Ian Carmichael aghast
School for Scoundrels was great
Classic humour, never surpassed

Glorious British comedy films
Designed to entertain
Black and white magic
That will never come again

Web of Deceit

I admired your silk construction
Unaware of the dangers there
I headed for the epicentre
Full of excitement, free from care

My instincts betrayed me
Mesmerised by your several eyes
I can't resist any longer
Oh keeper of the flies

Caught in your web at last
Arachnid devour me whole
Luscious and lascivious
Consumer of my soul

Pierce me where it hurts
Overwhelmed to be your prey
Inject me with your venom
Immobilised I'll stay

Your fang-tipped jaws are delicious
C'mon give me a kiss
Never knew that my destruction
Would end in the utmost bliss

Untimely Erection

Untimely erection
What more can I say?
Life in the old dog yet?
Hip, hip, hooray

But it's four o'clock in the morning
I don't understand this
No rhyme or reason
For a throbbing penis

Okay, let's be calm
Let's think this one through
Yesterday's adventures
Today, no longer hold true

So there's no point in fumbling
Trying to relive outdated extremes
Fantasies in your head
The best place, so it seems

Well, there we have it folks
The end of a very short story
I think in common parlance
It's called a morning glory

David Hardy

The Unkindest Cut

I was awaiting a surgical intervention
My nether regions to be invaded
A patient either side of me
Panic and fear pervaded

They were there for minor operations
Similar, but not the same
One fulfilling a religious obligation
The other ending a mating game

'I'm here for a foreskin circumcision', said one
My heart was full of dread
'It's a foregone conclusion', he muttered
I think that's what he said

'I'm a seasoned participant', said the other
'When it comes to genital upheaval'
'Vas deferens snipped vasectomy'
'But I decided for a retrieval'

'To reverse the clinical procedure'
'In order to have another child'
By now I was writhing in my seat
Agitated when he smiled

'I don't know what you're worried about', he continued
'It's time you realised'
'In the blink of an eye it'll be over'
'Trust me, you'll be surprised'

'Let me put it this way', he said
'There's a common misconception it's castration'
'But there's no room for having doubts'
'Only fifteen minutes duration'

And so I embraced uncertainty
My beloved member in my hand
Now an expert in a surgical procedure
Something I'd never planned

The Devil's Work

I hate arithmetic
With mathematics, I'm more adverse
Numbers are the Devil's work
Numeracy I do curse

I get the basic premise
Of addition, subtraction, multiplication
But cosines, algorithms and algebra
Are lacking in imagination

I'll not denounce percentages
Or the occasional fraction
Knowing how to be divided
Undoubtedly has an attraction

Don't bore me stupidly silly
With calculus and trigonometry
For I have words at my behest
To address this creative anomaly

Of course, everything now is metric
A hundred pennies in a pound
The Dow Index is up
Monetary theory to confound

Don't talk to me about measurements
Hands as well as feet
Centimetres replacing inches
Confusion is complete

Numbers are not like emotions
They can't be hidden or expressed
They're clinical and detached
Intrinsically suppressed

So, back to the Devil's work
The curse of numbers 666
Beelzebub's at work
Up to his old tricks

The Coldest Dish

I'd like to be a roll-on deodorant
Making an underarm advance
Keeping you dry and perfumed
Before ending this romance

I'd like to be a woodpecker
Chipping away at your head
Removing flesh, bone and blood
Instilling a sense of dread

I'd like to be a carpet fitter
Pulling a rug from beneath your feet
Rolling you up in linoleum
For a wheelie bin in the street

I'd like to be an intruder alarm
With a code that can't be remembered
Taking advantage of insecurity
Harmless now dismembered

I'd like to be an anomaly
A decidedly cold fish
There's something sweet about revenge
Consuming the coldest dish

Questions

Where are you from, my friend?
Have you travelled far?
What was your mode of transport?
Bus, train or car?

Are you still working?
Or have you now retired?
How do you fill your time?
What activities keep you inspired?

Do you have children, then?
One, two or three?
What are your children's names?
Do they live locally?

What was your career?
A tradesperson or office bound?
Did you enjoy your job?
Or did it get you down?

Have you enjoyed our conversation?
Do you think we should connect?
Do you think it's a bit too early?
Do you think I'm a bit direct?

Prince of Darkness

Don't confuse me with someone who cares
I'm fuelled by vacuous intent
I'm a vampire for your emotions
I feed off your discontent

You don't need to visit Transylvania
No need to make that trek
I'm just around the corner
Sizing up your scrawny neck

I'll sink my teeth into your flesh
Bloodletting for beginners
My position is intractable
I'm the prince of unforgivable sinners

It will take more than a crucifix
To protect you from all fear
Misery likes company
And company is very near

Just waiting in the darkness
A plump and crimson moon
Accompanied by my disciples
The conveyors of doom and gloom

So promise me you'll stay
Become part of the fraternity
Everlasting life guaranteed
And torment for eternity

(It's not) National Poetry Day

Flagged up, duly noted, message on display
Wisdom foretells many things
(It's not) National Poetry Day

Mistake made, easily played, fears yet to allay
Thank you for correcting me
(It's not) National Poetry Day

Facts explained, patience drained, little left to say
No longer does it bother me
(It's not) National Poetry Day

Getting up, playful pup, ready to greet the day
Another coffee, totally wired
(It's not) National Poetry Day

Finally conclude, time to move, now I'm on my way
Every which way you look at it
(It's not) National Poetry Day

LOVE

Far too vast to even contemplate addressing but suffice to say that for me it covers the deep affection I have, and have had, for friends, family and partners. Interestingly enough, my first poem ('Daffodils') was about the end of a relationship, and my favourite lyrics are from the song 'Love is Just a Four-Letter Word', written by Bob Dylan and performed by Joan Baez.

Daffodils

All the yellow daffodils
That bowed their heads today
Drenched in sun-kissed raindrops
Oblivious to the foray

Tamed but yet defiant
In contradictions of the heart
Like you and I in our coupling
Never far, but so far apart

The distance is so little
And my reality still sometimes sings
Of the friendship we shared together
Before immersed in our own things

You chose to be remote from me
I nearly drowned in my dismay
All the dreams of our youth we shared
Now lost in yesterday

A Fine Line

The conversation ran so freely
My fingertips caressed her hair
It was cinematography in my mind
For she was never there

Across a crowded room
Full of fellowship shared with grace
A shaft of broken sunlight
Lit up her porcelain face

Every line etched with pain
I have learned to memorise
I gazed at her fragmented perfection
A feast for my world-weary eyes

Maybe it is so wrong of me
Perhaps confession is better than fear
We are growing closer in understanding
Scared to lose what I hold so dear

Give it over to God on high
My conscience dictates to me
Let destiny takes it course
What is meant will surely be

No time to reflect any longer
On the rites of youth now past
Lifetimes that slipped through my hands
Relationships that did not last

So accept this gift with gratitude
In the knowledge she cares for you
And cherish what unconditionally exists
A friendship forever true

SWALK

You searched for it all your life
You tried to find the truth
The answers lie in the past
In the flower of your youth

You were so young and attractive
Before the years passed by
Your soft and radiant skin
And the twinkle in your eye

But you were so naïve
Raised a brood and built a nest
You were never a frontrunner
In the happy families contest

You regret not finding salvation
Through unity with another
Sought a caring lifelong friend
Above all, a soul brother

And so you start to reflect
It's a time to reminisce
Remembering those schoolyard days
Sealed with a loving kiss

Seasons

For you, I give everything
My heart that lost its way
The sunshine that melts the frost
On an unbecoming Winter's day

For you, I close my eyes
Fingertips caress the night
Tentatively growing together
In the dawn of early Spring light

For you, I will be true
My fire forever burning
Lazy hazy days
In the Summer of my yearning

For you, I am the one
With caring words unsaid
Laying down my Autumn leaves
A pillow for your head

Seasons of such variation
Arrive, as they must go
The love I have for you
Is all I need to know

One

Sunny days
Sensual ways
Lay down
Gentle sound

Purple heather
Entwined together
Soft flesh
Tender caress

Eyes wide
Now inside
Caring embrace
Special place

Inhibitions gone
Unconsciously one
Mystic vision
Spontaneous collision

Utmost care
Almost there
Final piece
Sweet release

Ecstatic expression
Joyful confession
Loving union
Sacred communion

Misspent Youth

I don't want to encounter a vagina
At this given point in time
I've been there before
Without any reason or rhyme

I guess it was to satisfy curiosity
But I'm no longer that way inclined
To engage in sexual activity
The blind leading the blind

It was always about fumbling around
In my considerably misspent youth
Trying to find a connection
Delusion versus truth

Ageing and atrification
They change your point of view
Embracing a lifelong friendship
The love that we daily renew

I was always open to suggestion
It took me years to realise
That love is a spiritual connection
Based on understanding and compromise

Kiss

Sometimes so alone
Though never really apart
Ever closer to the one
As ghosts of the past depart

Future seems so certain
Celebration in my sight
Emerging from the darkness
Immersed in the brightest light

Beauty without form
Inexplicable and undefined
Beyond our earthly conception
Defying analysis of mind

Found in a passing moment
A glimpse of eternal bliss
Like the innocence of an adoring mother
To the child a tender kiss

Dance

Laughing, skipping, singing
As you dance your merry way
Kindred spirits of good fortune
Watch over this child at play

Clouds from above disappear
As you're blessed by the Heavenly Son
Bringing smiles and tears of joy
To each and every one

Confusion and turmoil will arise
When you learn what you must know
That fairies, fondants, and daisy-chains
Are displaced as up you grow

So glide across the floor for Daddy
Let us cherish this moment we find
I love you my waif-like angel
With my heart, my soul, and mind

Dad Built a Boat

An engine from a Hillman Imp
Built with his own hands
Hull was made of fibreglass
To weather the sea's demands

Mackerel gutted on board
'Be careful of that sharp knife!'
Seagulls swooped incessantly
Purveyors of utmost strife

As a student, I worked at his business
The renowned Offerton Service Station
Took liberties as my father's son
Much to his consternation

A man of many dimensions
And untold complexity
Seldom a bad word spoken
And always there for me

People have different ideas
As to how we measure a life
A good man, without a doubt
Loved by Son and Wife

We'd change some things if we could
Damn that generational divide
Feelings rarely shared
And emotions kept inside

When I asked him about the afterlife
He said, as a rule of thumb
'It's easy to see, that Heaven to me….
Is being with you and your Mum'

Coal Miner's Daughter

Born in Philadelphia
Coal miner's daughter
Eventually snared an Englishman
Lamb to the slaughter

In the company of a nurse
Aged four she crossed the ocean
From America to England
Excitement and commotion

Settled well in Stockport
Visits to the Emerald Isle
Adventures in County Mayo
Horse-riding dressed in style

A former Adswood beauty queen
Cherished all the while
Cheekbones to die for
Arresting beguiling smile

Undeniably fashionable
Wore outfits like no other
Upstaged the entourage
Indisputably glamourous mother

Vigorously hated being old
Reluctantly acknowledged her fate
A note she wrote in her diary
'I'm past my sell-by date'

Wild, caring and humorous
A photograph seldom seen
Held in my hand this moment
The Adswood beauty queen

Angel Walk with Me

Childhood's end it heralded
Painful passage to adulthood
Erased those endless summers
Everything became misunderstood

Precious moments everlasting
Restored sweet memory
Across the straits of Menai
To the caravan by the sea

Essence of fragmented perfection
Innocence long since gone
Dreams no longer needed
For together we are one

Connected hand in hand
My return is now complete
To tender ways where I belong
United in our retreat

Special place of my rebirth
We walk the sandy beach
Our lives unfold in unison
Madding crowds beyond our reach

Oh my love I am so happy
When you are by my side
The sun slips into the ocean
Sacramental distant tide

Evening drawing near
The moon is riding high
Driftwood we have gathered
Stacked up and nearly dry

Crackling embers sparkle
Embracing warmth and liberty
Only one thing I ask of you
Angel walk with me

When I See You

When I see you in the morning
I'll convene a convenience of lies
That every dawn you'll be the vision
On which I feast my eyes

In my thoughts as day unfolds
Wishing to be gentled at your hand
I'll submit to a subterfuge of the truth
Always waiting at your command

As I hold you in the evening
My last vision of fading twilight
I'll dutifully despatch my distractions
To keep you with me throughout the night

Val's Poem

There she goes again
Casting her magical spell
With mesmerising activities
To get me through this lockdown hell

Accompanied by Eddie the dog
A canine companion who never fails
Ensuring every day
That a countryside walk prevails

Optimistic routines
An array of hidden pleasures
Not to be underestimated
I'm embracing daily treasures

Soon it will be lunchtime
And a board game is beckoning
Scrabble is my downfall
Another day of reckoning

Bruised and battered I emerge
To the welcoming smell of food
Evening meal is in the making
A delicious interlude

The weekends are particularly special
As the Breakfast Club convenes
I've never enjoyed such indulgences
Not in my wildest dreams

And so, it's the onset of evening
A TV murder mystery to be told
Forgive my occasional snoring
A stern rebuke is about to unfold

So, thank you for your special friendship
Each and every day
For overlooking my frailties
In your own special way

MENTAL HEALTH

Considering the number of people who have experienced
problems with their mental wellbeing, I'm amazed that it was
'brushed under the carpet' for so many years. At last (I think),
depression, anxiety and other ailments appear to no longer be
stigmatised. I've had my own 'ups' and 'downs', but sometimes
I write poems where I try to put myself in the shoes of another
person.

Withdrawal

I won't be defeated
At least not in this way
A victim of pharmacology
An experiment gone astray

The pain of withdrawal
Revokes any lasting hope
Barely surviving each day
Overwhelmed, unable to cope

The Sun, the clatter, the conversations
All inputs to my brain
Nothing makes any sense
On the perimeters of being insane

One good evening of sleep
Is something to which I aspire
Reclamation of normal functioning
Is all that I desire

Find me a health practitioner
Who understands the damage done
Of stopping medication completely
When there's a battle to be won

Unruly Thoughts Abound

Unruly thoughts abound
Messed up and masticated
Scraping from the barrel
Like a coconut desiccated

Should have addressed things sooner
As always, you vacillated
Now you're on the back foot
Emotionally deflated

And so you're confused
In the misty morning haze
Praying for clarity of mind
A correction of wayward ways

Unruliness is in your nature
The gnawing in your head
Logic dictates common sense
A place you fear to tread

Take it to the next level
When thinking is deterred
Reach out to those you trust
Be open, honest and heard

Temporary niggling doubts
Reaching the final frame
Reclaiming your self-worth
Relinquishing troublesome pain

Tomorrow

Time can hang so heavy
During a rainy Spring betrayal
The exhausting nature of greyness
Dullness and tedium to derail

It's no use blaming the weather
When there's something wrong inside
A day when you're weighed down
Unable to confide

The downward pull of gravity
Feels excessive this afternoon
Can't summon any enthusiasm
To leave the confines of your room

Rain is incessant but restrained
A contradiction you conclude
Completely disengaged
The lowering of your mood

Tomorrow you'll reconnect
And initiate a conversation
Embrace the world again
With hope if not elation

Suicide Prevention

This life you hold in your hands
Is too precious to throw away
Hard to envisage carrying on
Under a sky of foreboding grey

For some it's just another day
A sunny afternoon in June
Your heart is filled with darkness
Your default position is doom

There's nothing worth living for
In your self-loathing mindset
Everything is pointless
Tinged with a sense of regret

Negative self-talk prevails
Telling yourself those age-old lies
That oblivion is the answer
A solution with no goodbyes

You can't see a way out
A bridge or a bottle of pills
The futility of existence
An escape from all life's ills

Too immersed in your own malaise
To appreciate that help is there
That death at your own hands
Is a step beyond repair

So, reach out before it's too late
To a family member, a samaritan, a friend
For however bleak it seems
Now is not the end

Mental Health Awareness Week

Mental Health Awareness
I missed it the other week
I was feeling rather fragile
My future was looking bleak

Fifty-two weeks in a year
And only one is set aside
For incongruous Facebook postings
Mainly inconsequential, you decide

Remembering the enlightened Seventies
Embarrassed hush outside the room
Of a GP prescribing indifference
Foretelling a life of gloom

An anathema to the medical profession
A condition highly stigmatised
A 'pull yourself together' mentality
As no one ever dies. Do they?

A pep chat and some pills
A pharmacological solution
Cerebrally somewhat skewered
Behold the chemical revolution

It's more common than we think
A father to a son
'Come on you'll get over it'
'You're not the only one'

Hard to pinpoint precisely
Depression is complicated
For some it's circumstantial
Others are genetically fated

Let's make mental health a priority
A conference ten years ago
Nick Clegg espoused this objective
But progress has been slow

I wholly endorse the real crusaders
Those who campaign for change
Helping the sad, the lonely and abandoned
And those who are deranged

But mobile texting perplexes me
Clicking on this and that
Not making a real connection
Not engaging in real combat

If your mental health is challenged
You don't need online bullshit
Cut, paste and share
A pathetic and sad remit

The need if you are suffering
Is for support all year round
Face-to-face, not Internet driven
Empty mantras to confound

And don't think you're an ambassador
For something you don't understand
A cup of tea and sympathy
The blind led by the bland

So if you want to make a difference
Voluntary support might work
Stop sending me social media messages
For me they just don't work

Bipolar Street

Electric gate opens
Your BUPA-sponsored treat
Four weeks of mental gymnastics
As you enter Bipolar Street

Brain is fried and addled
Thoughts like solid concrete
You've arrived at your destination
The grounds of Bipolar Street

Used to be called manic depression
Now the revision is complete
Terminology is well understood
By patients of Bipolar Street

White coats and bedside manners
Downfall and defeat
A warm welcome is extended
By the nurses of Bipolar Street

Group therapy at 10 am
You reluctantly take a seat
Sharing your life with strangers
Disinterested of Bipolar Street

Time now is over
You make a swift retreat
Another speedy recovery
As you exit Bipolar Street

MISCELLANEOUS

This section of the book is really a cop out as it contains poems that I just felt unable or too lazy to categorise. Also, I love the word 'miscellaneous' which perhaps (along with 'random') could be aptly used to describe my personality. 'Must try harder. B minus, Mr Hardy.'

Fictional Exchange

'Acceptance is the key'
That's what he said to me
'Spirituality is something more'
'But understanding will set you free'

'That's easy for you to say'
Said I to he the master
'For tomorrow is nearly here'
'And what you have, I want faster'

'Count your blessings that you are here'
'And listen to what I say'
'Tomorrow will take care of itself'
'Just learn to live in today'

I couldn't sleep that night
Confounded by what he'd said
Then one evening the miracle occurred
And I slept soundly in my bed

A Different Kind Of Christmas

A different kind of Christmas
And I'm feeling rather cosy
Might push the boat out completely
And send a festive emoji

A different kind of Christmas
The tree is leaning – it's obvious to me
You rigorously refute this
Ah, the blessings of OCD

A different kind of Christmas
Primark shoppers sing to thee
In the midst of retail glory
It's underpants and socks for me

A different kind of Christmas
The high street is closed down
Hail Amazon Prime saviour
Jeff Bezos rides into town

A different kind of Christmas
Communication of such variety
Working in isolation
Embracing online society

A different kind of Christmas
Our trading partners lost
Politicians rhetoric abounds
Whilst we sadly count the cost

A different kind of Christmas
Consequences lie ahead
Of flouting pandemic rules
So a scientific adviser said

A different kind of Christmas
I want to embrace and hold
Those I miss so dearly
But for now I'll do what I'm told

A different kind of Christmas
And I'm filled with sad disdain
When the masses are still marginalised
And inequalities remain

A different kind of Christmas
For each and everyone
Yearning for a brighter future
In Two Thousand and Twenty-One

A Poem For Mike Garry

Talk, talk, talk
Let it radiate from within
Let words drip from the page
Let the spoken word begin

Let the imagination flow
Unhindered and inspired
Cranking-up creative energy
Enthused and totally wired

Give me a backdrop of music
The Cassia String Quartet
Poems of life in Manchester
Full of love, growing up, regret

Mike Garry with his 'Handwritten Miracles'
Electricity in the air
Eyes transfixed recounting stories
The artist, the creative stare

Give me more, give me more
More of the spoken tongue
The linguistic craftsman cometh
Strings, words and song

Talk, talk, talk
Let it radiate from within
Let words drip from the page
Let the spoken word begin

A Social Club

Lip synching feeling
Subtitled affair
Shades of Swedish noir
No emotion anywhere

Sat there in the corner
No handset to change the channel
Take me away to somewhere
Away from endless flannel

So many conversations
Perhaps I should join in
But it all seems so chaotic
My head is in a spin

Two couples then approach me
Relieving my consternation
I wonder if they know what I'm writing
I abandon expectation

And so I share some insights
It's time to spill the beans
From judgement to acceptance
All is never what it seems

Another Etymological Excursion

With utmost sincerity
Here are the basic facts
'Sin' means 'without'
'Cerus' denotes 'wax'

The origin of honesty
In marble monuments was born
Sculptors of utmost integrity
Crafting from dusk until dawn

Artisans who were genuine
Perfecting an ancient craft
Their endeavours lasting forever
Testament to thankless graft

Contrast with other craftsmen
Those who sought to deceive
Concealing cracks with wax
Exploiting the naive

Having nothing to hide
Not concealing the slightest flaw
A way of living for some
For others, I'm not so sure

Apricity

Sunshine on your face
The warmth, the chilling air
Exhaling frosted breath
Experience without compare

Stems from the Latin word 'apricus'
Meaning exposed to the Sun
Takes place in the coldest depths
When Winter has begun

More complex that a natural occurrence
It's the hope that begins a new day
It's the universe communicating
In a synchronistic and beautiful way

The simplicity of apricity
The subtleness of solar disinfection
It reminds us to be where we are
In the moment without direction

So, when you're out and about
On a clear, crisp wintry morning
Remember the exhilarating energy
When paradoxically the cold is warming

Billionaires

Self-made billionaires
Absolutism is here
Philanthropists turn in their graves
At this societal bum steer

Playground of the rich
Sending rockets into space
Submarines to the ocean bed
An unregulated disgrace

A situation that cannot be resolved
There's no answer to this malaise
The masses are anaesthetised again
Given over to the latest craze

The battles rage on
The war has been long since lost
Caring and conscionable communities
Ripped apart and truly quashed

Capitalism continues to be fêted
In the corridors of utmost power
Those with unimaginable wealth
Enjoying their finest hour

Damn them all, damn them all
Now is the time to dwell
For the love of the ordinary people
Let the billionaires go to hell

Usage and Abusage

'Abusus non tollit usum'
Misuse does not remove use
The improper application of language
There really is no excuse

Declaring war on bad grammar
A lexicographer came to fame
He wrote 'Usage and Abusage'
Eric Partridge was his name

A guide to good English
Published in Nineteen Forty-Two
Relevant to writers today
To the likes of me and you

A completely different interpretation
Could be given to this well-worn phrase
During interactions between acquaintances
When navigating a conversational maze

A person who is genuine
Could be openly applying usage
Whereas one with a hidden agenda
Might well be guilty of abusage

Nightmares

People, places and things
Inhabiting the depths of my dreams
Nightmares haunt dark nights
Revisiting dystopian themes

What does it all mean?
The sign of a troubled mind
Or the unconscious resolution of problems
Isn't that the way the psyche's designed?

Obscure clues and lack of context
The house is burning down
A sign of emotional upheaval
Dream interpreters have found

Trying to resolve the mystery
Piecing together an intricate jigsaw
Déjà vu springs to mind
We have all been here before

People, places and things
In my nightmares it makes no sense
Morning breaks again
Welcoming the present tense

Synchronicity

More than a series of coincidences
With a definite spiritual dimension
Synchronicity is rapture
Commanding of our attention

A philosophical perspective
No proof that it actually exists
It's the elevation of the human condition
Where meaningfulness persists

Coincidences that are acausal
Not governed by cause and effect
Our minds speaking to us in dreams
Across time and space, we connect

There is unity in diversity
Psychologist Carl Jung observed
Questioning our understanding
With plaudits well-deserved

Thinking of a long-lost friend
In that very instance, a telephone call
Connected with that friend again
The wonder of it all

Helpful signs from the universe
Outside mirroring the inside
Synchronistic spirits converge
External and internal worlds collide

Street Poem

This is a street poem
A poem about a street
Food vendors and concrete structures
Coffee shops where we can meet

Used to be a 'high' street
In days when things were orderly
Now it's an unholy refuge
A haven for the drunk and disorderly

No inner-city urgency
Not on this heralded street
Young people riding skateboards
Nike trainers on their feet

This is the story of a street
A street that is fine
Fit for a Sunday lunch
Bring your kids and a bottle of wine

This is the street
Where familiarity is the game
A thoroughfare for pedestrians
Where everybody knows your name

This is the street
A street where everything is mine
Suitably invested with decency
Where petitions are always signed

Used to live on a road
Welcome to my street
A great place to get acquainted
Really rather neat

Secret

A life-changing discovery
Many years ago, today
A family heirloom remains unrevealed
And that's the way it's going to stay

Some things are best kept secret
That's how it's meant to be
Some can weigh you down
Others might set you free

A skeleton in the cupboard
Foretelling your destiny
A roadmap for the future
Shrouded in mystery

An astonishing revelation
Emotions kept deep inside
Never to be given an airing
In whom would you confide?

There is some speculation
Conjecture on 'their' part
A secret you've carried so long
In the depths of your very heart

Piece of Cake

Thinking about sexual activity
It just came into mind
I didn't prompt it, nor indulge it
It was more of a cerebral find

Men and women (in those days)
And the complex chasm
Self-induced pleasure
Or a multiple orgasm (you wish)

Lots of discussion about it
The 'ins' and the 'outs'
Those who engaged regularly
And those who went without

Youthful exuberance
And libidinous surges
Discovering my inclinations
Satiating my urges

Looking back now
Young and slim, wearing blue jeans
Now I'm contemplating atrification
And wondering what it means

Formaldehyde

Blind dating, self-effacing
Eyes dilating, contemplating
Ideal partner
Soulmate for the taking
Animal desires, fruitful undertaking

Wined and dined, intertwined
Breach of etiquette, countersigned
Burgeoning relationship, undermined
Caged canary, completely confined
Out of sight, out of mind

Illicit connection, misdirection
Choice selection, close inspection
Minor adjustment, complete correction
Slight concentration
Rapt attention

Antagonism and bile, apprehension and retching
Spewing forth venom
Abdominal walls are stretching
Far flung emotions, in the moments you are resting
Hitherto engaging, now neither enticing nor arresting

A love that should have lasted
Should have been never ending
Insults that are hurled, offending and condescending
Another year of self-deceit
Of contention and contending

She used to be someone
With whom you could confide
Now awaiting her preservation
Suspended animation
In a jar of formaldehyde

Clichés

I hope you're sitting comfortably
You might find this hard-hitting
I'm tired of circular conversations
And endless hair-splitting

No point crying over spilled milk
A stitch in time, they say
Becoming insufferably complacent
Clichés our mainstay

It never used to be like this
What happened to you and me?
Growing old together indifferently
Is that the way it's meant to be?

The heady days are behind us
The anticipation is long since gone
Thought we were very well-matched
Never thought I'd be moving on

There is someone for everyone
Another cliché drifting in
When it comes to the relationship stakes
I always thought that I would win

Connections

I missed something today
Something passed me by
I'm only learning how to walk
When I should be flying high

And we still talk in tongues
Immersed in the spoken word
We don't need language anymore
In order to be heard

A loving glance, a smile
The acknowledgement of existence
Tearing down the barriers of enmity
Removing all resistance

The sky, the earth, the universe
No inhibitions, no restraints
Foretelling a different connection
Removing all constraints

Something's circling overhead
Showing us the way to go
Imbuing us with its wisdom
Giving us everything we need to know

Coronation Chicken

Jewel encrusted sceptres
Ceremonial staffs and rods
Shoring up inequality
Media fêted gods

Eulogised by the masses
Brainwashed to conform
Truth somewhat elusive
Accepted cultural norm

Democratic principles infringed
Through hereditary public position
Blood and death down the ages
Reprehensible feudal tradition

Historical perspectives aside
A family mired in shame
Consistently courting controversy
Whilst conveniently deflecting blame

Here's to abolishing the monarchy
One day a plot will thicken
Until then I'll remain
A coronation chicken

Petrichor

What is petrichor?
The sweet smell of rain on grass
Long lasting sunny days
That you thought would never pass

Fragrant release in action
From water on barren ground
A summer peculiarity
A perfume that hangs around

An ancient Greek derivation
'Petr' refers to stone
'Ichor' is a tenuous essence
Nature's own cologne

In the veins of the immortals
Golden fluid flows
Petrichor is mythological
The ancient Gods have imposed

Next time there's a downpour
And you're huddled in a tent
Remember petrichor is a complex word
More than an earthly scent

Discombobulated

Dis-com-bob-u-lat-ed
Conveying a sense of confusion
'Bobulate' is redundant
Etymologically, it's an illusion

A derivation appeared in print
In Eighteen Thirty-Four
Not to be confused with 'bumfuzzled'
Similar, but something more

Originated in the US
Enjoyed a fluctuating position
When Nineteen Sixteen arrived
Made a fully formed transition

A six-syllable marvel
To confuse, upset or frustrate
Synchronised bobbling about
In a disoriented state

Getting back to etymology
It's a hybrid without a doubt
A fun and fanciful word
We'd hate to live without

Drinking and Thinking

Drinking is the answer
If you're a working class person
It's a way to avoid reality
A calming, mind numbing diversion

Far too expensive
But the rich tax the poor
Alcohol keeps us at bay
It's a double whammy, that's for sure

And of course there's cigarettes
A packet of twenty or a cheroot
'A pint of bitter, please'
'And prosecco in a flute'

Maybe you'll transcend
The booze, the fags, the drugs
By adopting a twelve step programme
Self-abuse replaced by hugs

There you go again
Being obtuse and somewhat dense
Ignorance is bliss
Addiction, the perfect defence

Eddie the Dog (featuring Peggy)

Eddie the dog is out to play
A cursory glance, and then he's away
Running like the wind with Peggy at his side
A would-be groom for a wayward bride

And so we follow the daily routine
Throwing sticks and stones in a nearby stream
Watch him soar in the air catching pebbles in his mouth
Another photo opportunity, without a doubt

As the day unfolds, we return back home
Where he's free to wander and leisurely roam
Give him some attention and he'll be elated
His owner tells me I'm his uncle – it's nice to be related

The evening meal arrives and he wants your cuisine
To refuse to share some morsels would undoubtedly be mean
A rascal, a rebel – an affectionate rover
He's living the dream, forever in clover

Funeral Pyre

The time for living is now
Give it all you've got
Hell for leather, you bastard
Only earthworms when you're shot

Every single second counts
It's time for you to shout
Whatever your revolution
Never be in doubt

Okay, you're ageing by the moment
Well that's the way it's gotta be
All that really matters
Your enduring legacy

So get off your arse while you can
And don't give up the fight
Don't let the flames dwindle
Forever burning bright

Gotta tell you now
As we reach the very last verse
Gimme a blazing pyre
And fuck the funeral hearse

Page 274

A crime fiction novel
Coffee rings on page 274
Even the amateur sleuth
Deduced it had been read before

At the centre of this tale
A traditional domestic uprising
Three into two wouldn't go
Too much compromising

It all happened quickly
At about quarter to Eight
Caught them both together
Finally sealed her fate

The lover left the house
A violent argument ensued
She started to question his manhood
Not the wisest move

He lashed out uncontrollably
She flew across the hall
Quite balletic in her flight
Dining table broke her fall

Should have called for an ambulance
It was the right thing to do
Battered her to death
With the heel of her left shoe

Motionless and silent
No remorse, no despair
Limbs splayed out like a doll
Blood splattered hair

Reader interrupted by a colleague
Who just came into sight
Enquiring as to the sandwich filling
Brown bread or white

An appetite for reading crime
And for eating food, it has to be said
He put the book to one side
In readiness to be fed

Obsession

I'm hovering outside your home
Not the slightest bit afar
Watching your every movement
From the comfort of my car

Close physical proximity
Concealed but so nearby
You say we really connected
Disingenuous eye-to-eye

Now you are remote
Ignoring my utmost request
Regrets are everywhere
You're so easy to detest

Everything that we stood for
And all the things we lost
I condemn you to eternal misfortune
Forever you'll count the cost

Contradicting lessons of forgiveness
You inhabit my every thought
Death most certainly becomes you
My forgiveness cannot be bought

Mr Publisher

I'm all over the place
I love it
It's all the rage
A bit leftfield at times
Enter centre stage

Some people have presence
Stagecraft
It's not my thing
But in my naive way
I like the things I bring

Poems that deserve an airing
A public outing
One might say
Deserving of a bigger audience
To be aired in the light of day

Mike Garry
John Cooper Clarke
AKA JCC
My recent introduction
The best of performance poetry

Not something I aspire to
This stand-up kind of thing
Haven't got the talent
But here's something from the well
From the well the water will spring

To get better
According to the well informed
Those who know more than me
I need to read much more
Much more poetry

This I take on board
But I rarely do
Down the years of my existence
Books
I've only read a few

But I've got a body of work
Oh, yes
A body of heartfelt words
Humour, pathos, imagination
Words that should be heard

Please, please, please
Give me a chance Mr Publisher
Mr Publisher give me a chance
You're so difficult to connect with
With your stand-off creative dance

Modern Times

Where are we going?
I really just don't know
Unimaginable wealth
For admission to this show

It used to be so different
Cadbury, Rowntree and Leverhulme
There's no longer a moral compass
Philanthropists have left the room

Neoliberalism
Acknowledging the great divide
Should have renounced Thatcher and Reagan
Adopted Chomsky with utmost pride

I don't know much about politics
Oligarchs and billionaires
Where profit is all that matters
In a world of stocks and shares

Military Response

I don't like your personality
You're someone I detest
The emotional shots from my gun
Never breach your bullet-proof vest

You're undoubtedly an iron maiden
Rejecting my charm, I'll be damned
I can't penetrate your armour
With this broadsword in my hand

So I'll lay down all my weapons
I promise I won't come near
What a propensity you seem to have
For self-loathing coupled with fear

Let's stop this fighting now
Let me be loud and clear
Even if I marshalled an army
I'd never get very near

Mary Celeste

A merchant brigantine
Found adrift in 1872
Food and provisions aplenty
Absent were the crew

Suddenly, I could smell it, touch it, hear it
That palpable unrest
Troubled souls abandoned
Lost on the *Mary Celeste*

Discovered by a British ship
Captain Morehouse at the helm
Maritime malaise uncovered
Another time, a different realm

The ghosts of ten people
An abstract invisibility contest
Prayers for the forsaken misfortunates
Lost on the *Mary Celeste*

Changed owners many times
Reluctance to go on board
Particularly sailors on the high seas
Cursed reputation soared

Here I am again
Hear my crestfallen behest
Animation completely suspended
Lost of the *Mary Celeste*

Ended her days in the Caribbean
Run aground, left to fade away
Remnants of this enigma
Still remain to this very day

Just imagine being there for a moment
That sudden tightening in your chest
Mist overpowering your breathing
Lost on the *Mary Celeste*

A Bermuda Triangle for boats
In each and everyway
The past, the present, the future
A complex interplay

There was a time of fun and games
In the days when the ten were blessed
Before calamity claimed their lives
Lost on the *Mary Celeste*

Here's to those troubled souls
Finally left to rest
No longer lost, but found
Found on the *Mary Celeste*

Crazy Gift of Time

This crazy gift of time
An abundance for me and you
So many years ahead of us
And so much yet to do

Each day seems like an eternity
Basking in the midday sun
Schooled in the art of excitement
With races to be run

An education of sorts
Not a moment in which to wallow
Relationships to explore
Rewarding careers to follow

Births, marriages and mortgages
Endlessly counting the cost
Forever spinning plates
Not a second to be lost

Some people are off the radar
Whilst old friendships are rekindled
Thought there were many more
But they appear to have dwindled

All these foolish youngsters
Running around so bold
Contentment is what really matters
At least that's what I was told

Years blur into decades
An extension is fruitlessly sought
In the fibre of my being I know
That this gift cannot be bought

I've never felt this tired
And I don't sleep much anymore
There's an aching in my body
That I never felt before

Life doesn't last forever
I'm no longer in my prime
Thankful for the days I've had
For this crazy gift of time

I Really Do (Love You)

So many years, so many tears
Mistakes made in the past
So many dreams, so many schemes
Foundations that didn't last

Living in the moment now
Obliterating despair
Today affection exists
People I know who care

And you who stand aloof
Detached from raw emotion
All our days are numbered
Let's subjugate self-promotion

It's a one-way journey for everyone
For you and I, my friend
So let's be honest, open and heartfelt
Before we reach the end

So take it on the chin
For I have some news for you
After everything's been said and done
I love you, I really do

As Was Is

I was learning to be lonely
Each and every year
Afflicted with inertia
And a palpable sense of fear

I rarely initiated contact
Occasionally made a call
Socially uncomfortable
Self-doubt induced withdrawal

A dereliction of duty
Making isolation the norm
Just the way it's been
A failure to conform

Absorbed in a quiet moment
Thoughts I do dissect
It's always been like this
An inability to connect

I'm learning to reach out now
Coming out to play
Friendships I truly value
Growing closer every day

These Days

Stumbling along a side street
Wondering where you are
Pulling your soiled skirt upwards
Whilst flagging down a car

Maybe an open-air transaction
Or a visit to a shit-stenched room
Painful memories come to mind
Alcohol laced with gloom

Can't remember when you last washed
Deodorant-caked armpits
Skin pallor unbecoming
Endured too many hits

Body odour is rancid
Piss-stained knickers too
Clientele don't mind
Human beings who are through

During the 'act' of degradation
Arms outstretched, legs in the air
You try to remember a sunny day
When you didn't have a care

The ordeal is now over
As you venture out again
Tired, sad and lonely
Stepping out into the rain

Spiritually impoverished these days
Cursed by tortuous recollections
Standing back in line
While 'they' make 'their' inspections

Impression

Barefoot in the sand
Fingers in the snow
Resplendent and replete
Determining the way to go

Art movement depicting reality
Works of Monet and Renoir
Transient effects of sunlight
Permanent image, aide-memoire

Tribute band of quality
Retro glory chase
Sparks of genius fly
This nation's saving grace

Talent act of inconsequence
Mimicry on TV
Panellist votes are damning
Criticism given for free

First time you meet
In that moment it is fated
Long-lasting friendship
A connection understated

Imprints, pictures, imitations, and feelings
So many forms of expression
Always seeking a context
Within which to convey an impression

Humanity

Today's sermon is over
The congregation slowly leaves
I've never really questioned
What each and every one believes

They'll meet again next week
A few newcomers have remained
More wisdom to be dispatched
By those who've been ordained

One moment songs of worship
Then hushed words are spoken
Acceptance of the free
The lost, lonely and broken

It's easy to dismiss believers
In an age of self and disparity
I'll not be the one to condemn
Faith, hope and charity

The road I try to follow
Rejects all profanity
Accepts every faith
And embraces humanity

Happy 93rd Birthday, Lilian

The smallest of shooting stars
Two and a half pounds she weighed
A babe in arms indeed
Family members duly dismayed

Attended a school for fragile children
An infant full of charm
Kind, sweet, and mischievous
Always ready to disarm

After several years of schooling
From Summerseat House moved on
Fond memories of dearest Emily
A good friend long since gone

From the 'Jam-Jar' to 'The Catch'
Fishing with brother, Jim
Used bread and red worms as bait
Pickings were sometimes slim

Remembering days of old
In her poem 'Time Past'
The smog, the tar, the cobbles
The characters she amassed

With a voice like an angel
Lily didn't dilly dally
Singing songs of the age
Universally known as 'Sally'

Gordon was entranced
When Lily sang her signature tune
'Beneath the Lights of Home'
He was howling at the Moon

When Gordon made his move
Lily had lost her voice
He said he'd find it for her
She thought he was a good choice

Perhaps it was pre-ordained
Or a case of happenstance
But God smiled down that day
The beginning of a lifelong romance

When Pamela went to Canada
Overseas holidays ensued
Lily travelling on her own
Until later Gordon enthused

In the early Nineties
Lily attended a writing class
Sharpened her poetry skills
And 'The Memory Jar' came to pass

Writing about her children
And the avoidance of undue strife
Poems of good humour
Embracing family, friends, and life

With a love for nature's gifts
And a strong sense of community
Painted pictures to adorn her home
Relishing artistic opportunity

Immersed in her creativity
Always moving forward
Acknowledged as public-spirited
She was frequently rewarded

So, bring on today
Music and celebrations galore
Lily's 93rd birthday remembered
And here's to many more

Getting Away with Murder

A legalistic coupling
Latin words I fear
One is actus reus
The other is mens rea

A brief lesson in law
Not to be gifted daily
Maybe you've heard it before
On *Rumpole of the Bailey*

Both of the above are needed
When committing a crime you'll find
Actus reus is the action taken
Mens rea is your state of mind

For murder it's premeditation
When you've thought it all out
Manslaughter is somewhat spontaneous
Motivation is still in doubt

In order to avoid detection
Advice to each and every man
Murder is more calculated than manslaughter
And it's best to have a plan

Ministry of Stolen Moments

In the Ministry of Stolen Moments
Random thoughts like clouds pass by
Daydreaming is national policy
So much time to occupy

Parliamentary debates exorcised
In a free-thinking constitution
No self-serving politicians
Seeking absolution

Yes, in the Ministry of Stolen Moments
In the party of the people
Poets and dreamers are lauded
And everyone is equal

No time for vested interests
And lobbying has been banned
Communities are genuinely cared for
Love and truth go hand-in-hand

If you're seeking another department
And you're prepared to persist
Try the Ministry of Kind Hearts
An opportunity not to be missed

We're on the Move
(A POEM FOR MICK AND VICKY MIDDLES)

Abandoning Manctopia
Billion pound property tree
For a more authentic place
In the sight of White Nancy

Loading up a vehicle
From Cheshire Van Hire
Conjecture on the approach to be adopted
Starting to perspire

Arrived at our destination
Having given other drivers a wide berth
Manoeuvred through the traffic
Stayed patient, for what it's worth

What a fantastic dwelling
A truly inviting abode
Planning is earnestly in progress
In home improvement mode

Furniture from afar to shift
And stairs to circumvent
Carrying protruding shelving
Makes for a nervous ascent

With an expansive garden and awning
Raised beds and a spacious shed
Henry the dog can roam freely
As always, out of his head

A convenience store down the road
A leisure centre and community hub
And most important of all

David Hardy

Access to a traditional pub

Bollington's the place to be
For Mick and Vicky it's home
Mick will appreciate this quote
'Welcome to the Pleasuredome'

Undeniably Unreliable

Damn your inconsistency
Changed your mind again
Toing and froing indefinitely
Driving me insane

A beacon of unpredictability
I'll never come around
Not in this lifetime at least
Perhaps when I'm underground

Can't go on like this forever
Ready to launch my attack
Tired of being defensive
Now I'm kicking back

So I'll turn up as I do
At our usual meeting place
Lamenting your absence as always
Your unwieldy fall from grace

Guess I feel let down
Maybe it's a misunderstanding
Still love you unconditionally
Perhaps I'm too demanding

The Photographer

Everyday faces
Images to frame
Some people are constant strangers
Others you know by name

Every picture tells a story
A smile or a distant gaze
There is beauty and there's intensity
To bedazzle and amaze

Capturing life in all its stages
From childhood to old age
The youthful smooth-skinned rascal
To the wizened and wrinkled sage

Colours of exuberance
Radiating forth in broad daylight
Monochrome and moody
Camera obscura of the night

Always focusing on others
To freeze intimate moments in time
Anonymous faceless photographer
Self-ordained vicarious crime

The National Game

Cast your mind back
To a film of classic dimensions
Clipped ears, two finger salutes
And after school detentions

I never loved football
At least not truly madly
But I loved Brian Glover
And that pipsqueak, David Bradley

Dangling from the crossbar
With his shorts hanging down
Billy Casper was his name
His position was classroom clown

A kitchen sink drama
And a disarming sporting scene
Days of innocence and loss
The movie's enduring theme

It wasn't about tactics
Or pride before a fall
Just playing on a local field
Just kicking around a ball

Football was played for fun
Hero worship was for free
It had little to do with business
A bloodied nose and a twisted knee

Dribbling on the common
That was right up our street
Nowt to do with a Premier League
World at our very feet

Life has changed immeasurably
We'd be fools to deny the same
Even for those who don't like football
It was a passage, a ritual, a game

Denis Law was majestic
George Best beat all the rest
I appreciated the Sixties and Seventies
Everything since, I do detest

Still focusing on the great preoccupation
Life was less complex
No technology, no apps, no computers
Simplicity at our behest

I never liked watching football
But I enjoyed playing the game
Ken Loach's vision is broken
And things will never be the same

Ten Minute Poem

I no longer recognise you
You hardly look the same
Are you really the one?
The one I used to blame?

For all my misfortune
For the breaking of my heart
Reprisals in my mind
For tearing us apart

What a waste of precious time
So much out there for me
Instead I chose self-doubt
Overwhelmed by mediocrity

Built a wall around my being
Emotional penal servitude
Served an indeterminable sentence
Released for my good mood

And the realisation today
Is that I cannot live in sorrow
Opportunities await me
In the bright light of tomorrow

Tabloid Press

I read the news today, oh boy
This is plagiarism with intention
The headlines carried by the tabloids
Are unworthy of my attention

An unnamed television presenter
Until his identity was revealed
It's about bringing down the Beeb
Real story is always concealed

A minor news contribution
Playing their usual game
Always pointing fingers
Looking for someone to shame

The fascist media barons
The obscenity of the press
Careers and lives uprooted
Inequities to address

Real news is worth reporting
The marginalisation of the masses
Strikes and national unrest
The indifference of the ruling classes

Stories of war-torn regions
Suffering migrants who are rejected
Whilst scandal seeking editors
Wreak havoc with the unprotected

And as the wars continue
With the aim to maim and kill
The tour de force of *The Sun*
Is the titillate and thrill

Sunny Day In Scarborough

A cock stride from 'Tuthill'
Descending 'Long Greece Steps'
Enforcement Officer in a car park
Issuing his due respects

Entering a Bamford side street
Turning to the right
Boats, bars, amusement arcades
And novelty shops in sight

Mega balls in fluorescent colours
Giant furry aliens for sale
Bright, brash and garish
Rainbow rubbish will never fail

'Molly Malone's Fresh Seafood'
Crabs, prawns and kippers
Parental indoctrination of young ones
Feeding shrimps to expectant nippers

Motorcycles lined up
In a motorcycle zone
A biker tends a Harley Davidson
Before mounting his chrome throne

Ice cream gelato
'Award winning made in Filey'
The 'Silver Dollar Arcade'
Enjoying the life of riley

A prize every time you play
Always a winning break
Gifts galore you realise
Cheaper than your initial stake

Consumption is the name of the game
Aniseed and signature rock
Doughnuts and candy floss
Overhead, the seagulls flock

The Sun is absolutely scorching
Day tripping is the theme
Perhaps too many bodies
They'd be quotas under my regime

Couldn't get a drink
At the so-called 'Quayside Bar'
Rammed inside and out
Decidedly a step too far

Never seen so many people
Holding their drinks aloft
Macho beer-swilling antics
For the challenged and cerebrally soft

Finally found a craft pub
Now calm and composed
Exchanged chaos for conviviality
Infinitely predisposed

Stared out from 'The Frigate'
Drink in my right hand
My eyes fixed on a ginnel
Coastline, sea and sand

The beautiful harbour beckons
Deckchairs on the beach
Crab pots, sailing ships and day trippers
All readily within reach

And as I complete my outing
I bask in the warm sunlight
In a Victorian vision realised
That fills me with delight

Prestidigitation

Prestidigitation
A magical connotation

The usual sleight of hand
And a mind that is expanding
Perception and reality
Questioning understanding

Conjuring tricks are performed
Firing the imagination
Illusions and minor miracles
And audience participation

The Magic Circle, forever remains unbroken
And the secrets of the trade are never ever spoken

The gift of the magician
In a spectacle that is outstanding
The audience in his hand
He's convincing and commanding

Suspended upside down
By straitjacket and padlock
The time is ticking away
But he always beats the clock

The show finally reaches its natural conclusion
Enthralling onlookers with the ultimate illusion

And hands are held up high
With volunteers at the ready
A trick to top them all
The magician's hand is steady

An adrenalin-fuelled adventure
A woman is cut in two
The audience gasps in wonder
Another favourable theatrical review

Zombieland

Mannequins and models
Puppets and figurines
Matchstick men and women
Never questioning what it means

To be a remote automaton
Incapable of interaction
Your unwillingness to connect
Source of my dissatisfaction

There you stand indifferently
Pristine and unsullied
If you encountered an emotion
You'd probably be worried

Eyes glazed over completely
In a vacant unknowing stare
Conversationally you are impotent
You have nothing worthwhile to share

As I walk away from the huddle
Waving my right hand
There's no response from the living dead
From the inhabitants of Zombieland

Music

I cannot imagine living in a world without music. As a baby boomer, it's perhaps inevitable that I particularly appreciate music from the Sixties and the Seventies. I'm entranced by the lyrics of some popular music songs. The 'good' stuff, including Bob Dylan, Leonard Cohen and Richard Thompson, has influenced my own writing. Pop music, eh. It's all dross these days, innit?

Who'll be the Next in Line?

Idiosyncratic and somewhat bombastic
Both of these things you were
Your death in unusual circumstances
Created an almighty stir

Writing, recording, touring
Struggled to play the game
You never really grasped
The toxic nature of fame

Energetic, vital, urgent
A talent so sublime
Lyrics of such complexity
Your loss, a damnable crime

Hard living, drinking, drugging
Dogged your later career
Plagued with crushing self-doubt
Lurching from year-to-year

Excessive alcohol your downfall
Massive audiences you once drew
Alienated from friends and family
The occasional mixed review

With kindness, care and understanding
Could have been a different story
Fallen star now gone
No longer bound for glory

David Hardy

1976

Angry from Hemel Hempstead
Kicked the TV in
Grundy prompting anarchy
That sneering Lydon grin

Nineteen Seventy-Six
Or thereabouts I remember
If you're looking for exactitude
It was the 1st of December

Disaffected youth
Sterling crisis emerged
A musical revolution
Hippiedom duly purged

Archaic thinking challenged
And politicians' lies
I renounced the prog rock genre
Much to my surprise

Unashamedly I quote The Stones
'It's All Over Now'
Thank you to everyone who was there
It's time to take a bow

The Seventies

Nineteen Seventy was a good year
And I was only eleven
Educationally challenged
But still in seventh heaven

Arrived home from school
Knee grazed in a fight
Looked forward to a Vesta
And butterscotch Angel Delight

Black Jacks and Wagon Wheels
A scrumptious Aztec bar
Portions today are smaller
Nothing goes as far

Starman sang on television
'I leaned back on my radio'
Top of the Pops on Thursdays
The only music show

Platform heels and flares
Precursor to punk rock
Ideological revolution looming
A time for taking stock

Winter of discontent
Labour in poor health
Thatcher promoted a mantra
This is the age of self

Nineteen Eighty arrived
End of a great decade
If I'd known what the future held
In the Seventies I would have stayed

The Ballad of Nico

Innocent and vain
Wartime child of the lamp
Handing out food to Jews
En route to a concentration camp

She tried to outrun her background
Ashamed of her whole life
She never overcame the horror
The rage, the pain, the strife

Chiselled features and pale skin
The pursuit of a modelling career
A ticket out of Germany
Never escaped the fear

Had parts in several films
Fellini and later Warhol
La Dolce Vita and *Chelsea Girls*
Nothing could make her whole

An infamous affair
With French star Alain Delon
Just another port in a stormy sea
Yielded her only son

Dylan wrote her a song
'I'll Keep It With Mine'
She recorded the song herself
Heartfelt by design

Her fifteen minutes of fame
Her moment of crowning glory
When Warhol undermined the Velvet's
A complex and chequered story

Despite the tension that existed
Between the chanteuse and the band
'I'll Be Your Mirror' was written
Flowed freely from Lou's right hand

'Lawns Of Dawns'
The first song she ever crafted
Self-penned intensity
Comfort zones impacted

Genre defying Avant Garde
Gothic and full of gloom
Atmosphere of a broken childhood
Poison Ivy, sweet perfume

There is no hope, only despair
No matter whom you befriend
The theme of her work, as always
Was exemplified in 'The End'

She inspired many musicians
Siouxsie and The Cure
Bauhaus and Elliott Smith
And many, many more

Moved to Prestwich and Salford
Towards the end of her days
Addressed her heroin addiction
Embracing healthy ways

Described rather tellingly
As 'half goddess, half icicle'
Died aged forty-nine in Ibiza, Spain
Tragically falling from her cycle

Spent the whole of her short life
Staring into the depths of despair
Reflecting it back to her audience
A mirror without compare

A flawed but compelling human being
Who was buried in her mother's plot
Experienced humanity at its darkest
Gone but not forgot

Strummercamp 2023

Friday evening seven o'clock
Said 'hi' to the folks on the door
A couple of bands this evening
Tomorrow, many more

A smiling volunteer
The genie has left the lamp
Carrying an enduring message
Forever Strummercamp

Chatted with a stalwart
'You know when you've arrived'
'In this moment you have landed'
Sentiment uncontrived

Crescent moon illuminates
The club house down below
Stillness of night is broken
By a powerhouse of a show

The sound of the Ramoaners
Preceded by Cool Confusion
Vibrant and visceral
Rock and punk infusion

The evening is coming to a close
Friday's end is almost in sight
I'm thinking 'bring on Saturday morning'
As I walk into the night

Tents erected at random
For people to freely camp
Friendship overflowing
Forever Strummercamp

Saturday morning seance
To raise me from my slumber
Cranium thumping rhythmically
Self-induced thunder

Something of an incantation
But not in the slightest bit slick
'Made with love, (they say)
(And) sealed with a kick'

Achingly impossible?
A dream fully realised
Musically engrained wisdom
Highly politicised

'A real game changer'
Said a punk with a searing glance
'Police and Thieves' he uttered
Adopting an anti-racist stance

It's a gloriously sunny evening
When Jah Wobble turns up his amp
With The Invaders of the Heart
Forever Strummercamp

Cranking-up the music on Sunday
Hard core punk and reggae
Shifting from one genre to another
A comfortable segue

'A Part of No Tribe'
(My Life Through One Thousand Singles)
The author is affectionally interviewed
Aficionados gently mingle

This musical discussion continues
Between Four Candles and Mick Middles
Drawing from a well of anecdotes
Mixing reverence with impromptu giggles

'It's a murky world indeed'
And I have no affiliation
With people exuding falseness
The lost souls of this nation

No words are left unsaid
Nothing to revamp
These are heady days my friend
Forever Strummercamp

You cannot shackle dreams
Forever floating free
Singing songs of freedom
Please hear my soliloquy

Hands join in the redemption circle
In a show of goodwill and unity
A genuine moment of affection
An outpouring of humanity

And as we watch the setting Sun
As we've done so many times before
Here's to connecting again
At Strummercamp 2024

Signatures of approval
Sealed with a socialist stamp
Here's to our fraternity
Forever Strummercamp
Forever Strummercamp
Forever

David Hardy

Really Free

The Aylesbury boys are back
Reconciled at last
After fifty years of on and off
Finally having a blast

Said Willy in good humour
'Here we are, fifty years in'
Otway's musical virtuosity
Now extends to the theremin'

Took me back to 'Whispering Bob'
And *The Old Grey Whistle Test*
Cheese and toast at the interval
Of a late night music fest

Finally hit the charts
With the memorable 'Really Free'
Appeared on *Top of the Pops*
The epitome of eccentricity

Supremely optimistic
With everything to gain
Relished every moment
Of their fifteen minutes of fame

'Beware of the Flowers'
Should have been their second shout
Not the B-side of 'Really Free'
Bad decision, without a doubt

Went their separate ways
Otway's 'pop star' singular vision
Willy a multi-instrumentalist
A rather accomplished musician

Working the audience tonight
The atmosphere is electric
Otway and Barrett
Still wide-eyed and eclectic

Over 40 Years Have Gone
– Twas A Long Time To Wait

Never been to Prestwich
Nor Bury New Road
Haven't drunk at The Forester's Arms
Where Mark E famously crowed

Never saw the Buzzcocks
The Drones or The Fall
Missed going to The Electric Circus
And the legendary Free Trade Hall

Never listened to Ian Curtis
And members of Joy Division
Renaissance in my thinking
Complete and utter revision

Never attended a gig
By a man in a paper mâché head
Didn't witness his creative genius
Just listened to what people said

Never really appreciated
Tony Wilson's visionary perspective
New Order, Factory, The Hacienda
Complex business directive

Now I really value
Punk and new wave history
But why I wasn't there
Is something of a mystery

Anyway, it's not just the music
Poetic Mancunian spark
The brilliance of Mike Garry
The one and only John Cooper Clarke

Decades have passed me by
Still many flowers to pollinate
Over 40 years have gone
Twas a long time to wait

Musical Recollections

From Sister Rosetta Tharpe
And a heart full of soul
To an icon from St Louis, Missouri
A pioneer of rock 'n' roll

From a kind of blue
To a love supreme
Trumpet and saxophone in unison
The ultimate jazz dream team

From a Liverpool band of repute
Where swooning girls would moan
To the voice of a generation
Bringing it all back home

From an Avant Garde protagonist
And a rock-n-roll heart
To the seminal banana sleeve
Warholian experiment in part

From the cork-screwed hair of the star
Who rode a white swan
To the wide-eyed boy from freecloud
Cracked actor at number one

From down by the jetty
By proto-punk pub rockers
To God save the Queen
From anti-establishment shockers

From unknown pleasures
To power, corruption and lies
New wave, post punk, electronica
A singer's untimely demise

From flowers in a back pocket
Gladioli misappropriated
To the passage of forty years
Endlessly curated

Moving On

There's a hushed kind of reverence
For the post-war incoming tirade
Young people rejecting authority
Unbowed and unafraid

The Teds, the Mods, the Rockers
Perpetuating anti-establishment themes
Pasty-faced teenagers
Living out their dreams

New Wave insurgency
Challenging the great divide
Anthems of discontent
Ideologies cast aside

Ageing music aficionado
Still got all the clothes
The Damned t-shirt under his jacket
Emblazoned with New Rose

He looks a bit weary
Resignation in his eyes
The energy that existed
The wonderment, the surprise

Everything's been closed down
Youth movement is restrained
No point in being rebellious
When there's nothing to be gained

Consumerism has taken over
Prey to media lies
Only individual aspirations matter
In a world of compromise

Johnny Tillotson

He handed me a piece of paper
Because he knows I like to write
The pressure of developing a theme
On what essentially could be shite

All is pretty weird
Why does he do it to me?
A name on a piece of paper
A singer of obscurity

On the paper there was just a name
The name was Johnny Tillotson
'Poetry in Motion' he sang
Two weeks at number one

And he coined the phrase unknowingly
It didn't exist before the song
The origin of beauty and connection
A place where we belong

Written by Mr Anthony and Mr Kaufman
In innocent and challenging days
The state of the earth was fragile
In the heat of the cold war malaise

It was Nineteen Sixty-One
Ray Charles and Ben E King
Suicide no longer criminalised
If suicide is your thing

Life full of adventure
Innocence and commotion
Elegance, lightness and fluidity
'Poetry in Motion'

Joe Strummer

God bless Joe on high
And all he represented
Socialism and equality
Fuck the misdirected

Those who were taken in
Fooled by Tory lies
Time for taking action
No room for compromise

There was magic on the airwaves
A Radio Clash eruption
Crooked politicians
Self-interest and corruption

He roared like a lion
The loudest in the pride
A humanist by nature
Three amigos by his side

Rocked against injustice
Racism and detention
Supported striking miners
Encouraged mass dissension

Constantly at odds
With a major record label
Suppressed creative output
Cards upon the table

There are Clash songs in the ether
In the Hammersmith Palais
The world is still worth fighting for
When we step into the day

But nothing ever changes
No uprising in these isles
The Mescaleros frontman
Still denouncing Tory bile

Bhindi Bhagee and Johhny Appleseed
A barometer for right and wrong
Changing lives forever
Singing a Redemption Song

Remember December
In the year of Two Thousand and Two
The warlord sadly passed
Leaving a legacy for me and you

Twenty years since his death
And the corporations have all cashed in
Selling a back catalogue of conviction
Committing the cardinal sin

Of advertising cars and phones
To the materialistic consumer set
Inequality still exists
Post Thatcherite regret

There's a mural in Rastafarian colours
In red, yellow and green
The future is unwritten
And the truth is seldom seen

Field Commander Cohen

A television interview from yesteryear
On prime time morning TV
The guest was Field Commander Cohen
Holding court linguistically

'What do you value most?' he was asked
Said he 'The voluptuousness of austerity'
'The sensual gratification of simplicity' he continued
Disarming and filled with temerity

This was my first encounter
With the indomitable verbal gymnast
An indelible impression was made
And a magical spell was cast

Poet, writer, philosopher
Recording 'Death of a Ladies' Man'
Crafting songs in a 'Chelsea Hotel' (# 2)
Singing 'So Long, Marianne'

Those sultry smoky eyes
And that deadpan baritone voice
Seduced by his warmth and intellect
Drawn in without a choice

Smouldering with absolute charisma
He held beauty in the palm of his hands
Like moths around a flame
Women flocked to meet his demands

Dark lyrics and social unrest
Covering faith, regret and immorality
Romantic and sexual love
The nature of life and mortality

He 'straddled artistic borderlines'
According to a US publication
A renaissance man undoubtedly
Worthy of investigation

Time to make up your own mind
And don't let anyone fool ya
As the complex genius once sang
It's a cold and it's a broken hallelujah

Factory Music Radio

'Her name is Rio
And she dances on the sand'
Lyrically inconsequential
Musically somewhat bland

Just another track
From a factory music radio
Killing the sound of manufacturing
Of production in full flow

Something to help drown out
The vibrations of the mill
The irony of The Jam
Singing 'The Bitterest Pill'

Industrial noise overwhelmed
Thumping cacophony cast aside
Beating white hot metal panels
Stomach churning deep inside

Every single day
Factory music radio in your head
Facing Monday mornings
With a heart full of dread

You can't do this anymore
The heat, the toil, the sweat
Time to consider your options
In your ways becoming set

You down tools in that moment
In the background a familiar tune
You negotiate with HR
A leave date in mid-June

Into the unknown you go
Now you're going with the flow
So happy to leave behind
Factory music radio

Now you're a home worker
Enjoying being alone
Relishing the occasional interruption
Of a ringing mobile phone

Sometimes you like to sit
In the silence of the Moon's glow
The only thing you'll never miss
Factory music radio

NATURE

I'm blessed by easy access to the countryside, and I spend time walking along a canal contemplating my navel and being irritated by someone or other. It's in moments when I truly value my surroundings that poems come to mind, both the grandness of it all ('Forever') and the minutiae ('Dandelions').

Forever

Sweet times are coming
Winter is in retreat
Gravel breaks the silence
Crushed beneath my feet

Walked along the towpath
Meandered for several miles
Saw couples hand-in-hand
And strangers exchanging smiles

Sun lit up the hillside
Through the grey foreboding sky
Clouds edged with silver threads
Were slowly passing by

A child was quietly playing
From his hand breadcrumbs released
Impatient geese awaiting
Looking forward to a feast

All manner of waterborne craft
By the canal side they were tethered
Reminders of an industrial age
Iron cladded and weathered

Kinder Scout in the distance
Observed by the lucky few
A paradise for ardent walkers
A truly majestic view

Rain has replaced the sunshine
It's time to head for home
A wish that won't materialise
Is that forever I will roam

The Sun Beats Down on Shaldon

Searing, raging inferno
Makes for a special occasion
Vision fragmented and blurred
Retinal solar invasion

Shafts of sunlight dancing
Shimmering on the street
Paving dripping with silver
Heat beneath bare feet

Cottages casting shadows
Along the ginell to the right
Towards the picturesque bay
Still hot, but not so bright

Normal eyesight reinstated
Benefitting from shade
Colour and definition restored
Time for an escapade

Shaldon to Teignmouth by ferry
Across the sandy beach
Another adventure looms
Easily within my reach

Tentative Inclination

An inevitable descent
With aches and pains to follow
A sense of achievement is assured
In the scrutiny of tomorrow

In the meantime I'm moving upwards
From the basecamp of William Clough
Marshalling inner resources
I'm made of the sternest stuff

The Sun beats down relentlessly
As the summit is finally reached
My hear beats like a hammer
And my hair is slightly bleached

I asked a seasoned walker
Whether I was now on Kinder Scout
He addressed my reservations
And eliminated my self-doubt

I explored the topography
For me, unfamiliar terrain
So much there to explore
So I'll be going there again

David Hardy

Sun-Induced Inertia

Sun-induced inertia
Productivity undermined
Brushed it off in your heyday
Not so easy, now you find

You thought it would be a cinch
Finding the right words to say
Extreme heat clouds the mind
Communication goes astray

Conversation is curtailed
Words are barely spoken
Utterances of goodwill
In the main are merely token

Breaking into a sweat
Overcome by perspiration
Copious amounts of water
To subjugate dehydration

Beetroot red face
In the shadows, should have stayed
Lured by the promise of a suntan
Once again, you've been played

All colours are pastel shades
Too bright to be clearly defined
Squinting at the Sun above
Day off work has been countersigned

The car door handle is hot
And so is the steering wheel
Two for the price of one
Something of a steal

Three weary roadside workers
Laying down a track
The smell of bubbling bitumen
Hoping never to come back

A young lady passes by
Dressed in a polka dot frock
A throwback to the Nineteen Fifties
Time to reset the clock?

Dogs panting heavily
Drinking from water bowls
Retreating to the great indoors
To avoid walking on hot coals

Apartment blocks and paving stones
The smell of burning skin
Bare feet on scorched ground
Maybe it's time for staying in?

Sun-induced inertia
We're victims of vacillation
But onward we do go
Fuelled by obligation

St Anne's on the Sea

Welcome to the dog walkers paradise
A pleasant peninsula to roam
Occupied by indigenous species
Many beaches to happily comb

An over nourished adult
An Adonis in his mind
A saucy seaside postcard
Self-deluded I think you'll find

Erecting a wind breaker
'Can I help you with that bro?'
In common parlance they're brothers
Biologically, I just don't know

As I walk along the beach
I see a picket fence
A toothless structure indeed
Offering little or no defence

To my left, the shallow sea
To my right, Blackpool Tower
Remembering the illuminations
And the occasional winter shower

A father flies a kite
Pink, yellow and blue
Arrested by the colours
A gift for me and you

Sky Bright

I'm not seeking much these days
Simplicity's the way to go
No pot of gold exists
At the end of this rainbow

A spectrum of colours unleashed
Diffused by a rain-drenched prism
Elements conspire together
Instantaneous, atmospheric collision

Chaotic creation of beauty
Incoming storm below
Cymbals orchestrally crashing
Fragmented, theatrical plateau

Retreating from the downfall
And the onset of the night
Silver shafts exploding
Grey sky set alight

Invariably the moment passes
A gift that takes me higher
The Sun creeps into view
To re-energise and inspire

Shifting Seasons

Apple white, cherry red
Blossoms in your gaze
Beauty consigned to memory
Time will not erase

Blue skies, ivory clouds
Orange globe, scorching rays
Sensitive skin
Sun-filled days

Copper-bronze, speckled yellow
Carpeted forest floor
Grab a leaf, make a wish
Hope for something more

Grey, watery landscapes
Skeletal trees prevail
Fires warm frozen bones
Blessed are the frail

Out of Season

Staying at Star Cottage
Next door to the Shipwrights Arms
Situated in Shaldon
Full of Devonian charms

Mist descends on Teignmouth
Estuary is obscured
Old haunts to revisit
New places to be explored

Rain beats down in buckets
Sky and sea collide
Waves crash on the horizon
Summoning the incoming tide

Day trippers out for a walk
With dogs along the beach
Holiday season beckoning
Just outside our reach

Multi-coloured cottages
Pink, yellow and white
Yachts and sailing boats
Seagulls in full flight

Jam and clotted cream
In conversation, immersed
Buttered scones with raisins
Earl Grey to quench our thirst

Weather won't impede our progress
Out and about we'll be
Ensuring our daily excursions
Are consigned to memory

Mid Afternoon Sun

Blue sky, no clouds, only jet streams
Shadows of birds flying high
Coaxing the sun, winged tempters
Feathered collective passing by

The crackling of solar flares
As the ancient fireball dances
Reflections from a waterborne mirror
Unleashing nature's advances

White-walled cottage and magnolia
Heat and light converge
Early Spring casts its spell
Essential sunlit energy surge

People in the street illuminated
Everyone is moving slow
Days like this last forever
Tell me this is so

Sun-struck and transfixed
A song is happily sung
Captured in the moment
As you were when you were young

Lyme Park

Walking in Lyme Park
The sunniest day as yet
To be anywhere else today
Would fill me with regret

A canopy of utmost charm
Sun-infused and emerald green
Translucent umbrella
Such beauty seldom seen

Looming on the horizon
The glorious Lyme Hall
Welcoming visitors from afar
To engage and enthral

Up the stairs of the sandstone cage
Where ladies used to gaze
At the stealth of the stag hunters
Outmoded historical ways

Jackdaw swoops down
To a fold-out wooden chair
At the table of a family
Sweets and savouries left to share

A group of marathon runners
Exchanging their best times
Seemingly self-absorbed
Committing conversational crimes

Looking beyond the Park
Towering structures in the distance
Clocked some familiar landmarks
Grateful for my persistence

End of an enriching journey
Precursor to many more
Wondering what is next
What adventures lie in store

Food for the Senses
(ANOTHER CANAL WALK)

Early morning Spring walk
Puddles in which to tread
Jackdaws screech in unison
Clearing the cobwebs in my head

I screw up my eyes so tightly
To see a steeple in the distance
I pat the dogs of walkers
With little or no resistance

All hands on deck
In readiness for the mallard flight
From canal runway to thermals
Overhead and out of sight

Eyes down and synchronised
Sheep collectively grazing
Never diverted from their mission
Really quite amazing

Chimney smoke from a barge
Engine purring sweetly
Nervous dog protects the helm
Pleasures enjoyed discreetly

Slipped at bridge 24
Could have avoided the puddle
Always the same, I should refrain
Unnecessarily inviting trouble

The watery sun is rising
Lighting up the bushes below
Evergreen and ever ready
Emitting a sun-kissed glow

Carefully managed hedgerows
Skeletal budded trees
Tempted by the promise of Summer
Invariably bound to please

Reflection of the trees is broken
As geese invade the canal
A heron asserts its fishing rights
Temporarily breaking the spell

Emerald green lichen
Inhabiting a dry stone wall
Nature's ultimate goal
To bewitch and to enthral

Scenery to reinvigorate the senses
Food to fill the hole
A season of unspoken healing
Restitution of the soul

Dandelions

Plucked a single flower
Lips in puckered position
Took a sharp intake of breath
Collaborated on a mission

To launch a flurry of parachutes
On a journey pre-ordained
I exhaled with all my might
Only stems and leaves remained

Perfectly honed creation
Delicate, fragile and frail
Nature's architectural wonder
Is scattered along the trail

Grasped another dandelion
A seed head in my possession
Getting the hang of this game
My latest floral obsession

Held on to my burgeoning guests
Wished for the best of fate
Blowing more of the aforementioned flora
Several wishes to now collate

David Hardy

Coves

Catacombs, labyrinthine, esoteric by design
Open mouthed, eyes watching
Since the beginning of time

Secretive, beguiling, mystery to unravel
Trepidation exists, add caution to the mix
Pay heed to when you travel

Foreboding, unpredictable, all-consuming sea
Coastline scattered, sailing craft shattered
Waves crash down relentlessly

Tentative, beleaguered, weather warnings prevail
Tide times, limited confines
Sailing plans derailed

Disappointed, unsatisfied, lowering of self-esteem
Puzzles remain, secrets maintained
One day you'll fulfil your dream

Birdsong

Sunburst subdued
By silver and grey motif
Strangely illuminated landscape
Images in relief

Darkness claims the moment
Cloud surround, final push
Librarians of the skies
Custodians of earthly hush

Silent and still
The birds have gone to ground
Obliteration of the senses
Of sight, and of sound

Thunderclap breaks the tension
In a meteorological surge
Light emission reassures
Birds ready to emerge

Brightness of day reclaimed
Ethereal undertaking
The birds have just returned
Singing songs of their own making

Reminisce

Even as a relatively young person, I was interested in the past.
Not British or global history, but personal experiences, places,
friends and things. It is as if the past can occasionally be a
warm blanket to comfort one from the rigours of the moment.
By no means was the past perfect, but it's nice to bask in fond
memories.

Young and Foolish

How are you, my love?
I'm sure you know the score
I've loved you since time immemorial
And before the days of yore

Nothing compares with your beauty
Every word you ever spoke
Spare me from the weather
Keep me warm beneath your cloak

Preoccupied by thoughts of you
Submerged by the incoming tide
Sharing our lives together
You and I, side-by-side

Sitting on park benches
During long lost Summer days
Innocence remembered
Before struck by a malaise

Everything passes eventually
People change and grow
A stranger now in my midst
Someone I used to know

Climbing

There you stand at basecamp
At the coalface of humanity
Surveying the journey ahead
And the avoidance of calamity

Sights firmly set on the future
And it's a long way to go
Elements and emotions
The rain, the Sun, the snow

Is it the end game that matters?
Reaching the summit way on high
Or the fellow adventurers you meet
Whilst reaching for the sky?

You're climbing through the clouds
Your destination now in sight
The air is cold and thin
And the future is no longer bright

If only you'd understood
You didn't need steely determination
All you needed was love
And a basecamp explanation

Canal Encounter

Skull and crossbones flag
Uncomfortable juxtaposition
Canalside birds singing
Minor act of derision

Pushed through the water insistently
Lydon moniker on the boat
Flag flying in the breeze
Defiant and remote

Chopping guitar chords
Long since heard before
Emerging from the helm
The familiar 'I Fought the Law'

I engaged in conversation
With a couple called Sally and Pete
Two steadfast punks from Manchester
Nicer couple you could not meet

Pete and I shared some commonalities
As the Sun shone even brighter
Just a few moments of simpatico
Between lyricist and aspiring writer

When The World Was Young

Not a word, only silent grimacing
With pebbles beneath bare feet
Descending the winding path
On the annual Summer retreat

End of the journey he leaps
Released from stones of despair
Lands flat-footed in the sand
Arms flailing in the air

Open hands are throwing outwards
His bucket and his spade
A stream nearby meanders
Sandcastles soon to be made

Hair is mousy and tousled
Frame is bony and lilywhite
Seagulls on Puffin Island
Sky bound scavengers in his sight

He runs like the wind towards
The welcoming shimmering sea
Angels overhead are witness
To the day when he was free

What is Young Love?

What is young love?
Couples hand in hand
Piggybacks on the beach
Love letters in the sand

What is young love?
Saturday morning cinema features
Cuddling in the back row
Away from prying teachers

What is young love?
The heightening of the senses
First kiss on the lips
The lowering of defences

What is young love?
It's nurturing and attention
A youthful rite of passage
A human intervention

What is young love?
An incendiary device
Sparks only occur once
On the rare occasion, twice

What is young love?
Fleeting and oh so sweet
Innocence cast aside
Young love is now complete

Traeth Bychan

Tumbling down the embankment
At our favourite caravan site
Racing sticks in the babbling brook
Imaginations set alight

Inevitably things have changed
Gone is the gift shop on the beach
Knickerbocker glories and candy floss
So easily within our reach

Fond memories of the sailing club
Basking in solar flares
Soaking up the moment
Abandoning all cares

Blessed with good fortune
On this bright and sunny day
Strange how it seems so small
I don't remember it that way

Evening is drawing in
The fire begins to burn
Moon illuminates the tide
One day we will return

Sage Advice To Oneself

Can't reclaim one's innocence
Draw naivety from the well
The past is a foreign country
And not a place to dwell

Sure you made some errors
More than the odd mistake
It's in the nature of being human
Give yourself a break

Be selective with your memories
Don't let the bad ones bring you down
The clock goes back to zero
When tomorrow comes into town

And as the new day dawns
With birdsongs in the wings
Cherish each passing moment
And the contentment that it brings

Looking through rose-tinted glasses
So you may surmise
But every day is precious
No time for compromise

Reflections

Revisiting those times and places
Your yesteryears and todays
The challenges you overcame
Young person yearning praise

Now questioning the sacrifices
Those made in earnest pursuit
Of dreams that appeared worth chasing
That no longer seem to compute

A restless evening passes
Thinking about tomorrow
What's it all about?
Maximising happiness, minimising sorrow?

Friends, lovers and family
Who entered and left your life
You'd probably do it all again
The chaos, the mayhem, the strife

The dawning of realisation
Age is the counterpoint to youth
Time is slipping away
As you finally accept the truth

Generations

There's a feeling of wellbeing
A feeling everywhere
A preoccupation with hopefulness
An abandonment of despair

Reading jokes on lolly sticks
Watching toy balloons passing by
Candy floss at a funfair
A prize from a coconut shy

Memories of childhood remain
As if it were yesterday
'Time to grow up my son'
My father used to say

I never understood his view
Perhaps a post-war perspective
An aspirational end game
A working class directive

He certainly had a point
This, I cannot deny
But I wanted something more
I was reaching for the sky

So find me dancing under the moon
See me meld into the night
In flight above the oceans
Forever burning bright

Fool's Paradise

Do you remember Dialy?
Also known as Dialstone School
Hardly a seat of learning
Messed up this old fool

Tried to avoid detention
In fabricated confines
The unruly gathered together
Fate of a thousand lines

Safety there in numbers
Camaraderie sometimes existed
Eschewed mathematics completely
A subject to be resisted

Corporal punishment practised
By teachers baying for blood
A ritual of growing up
'Never did no one no good'

Institution to remember
Archaic rules prevailed
Any fond recollections?
Now that this ship has sailed

Could Have Been Me

There are those whom I truly envy
In the great wide world out there
Pursuing life most vigorously
Getting by without a care

On the subject of discomfort
They never really bled
They never felt the pain, the suffering
Of loving words unsaid

They had it every which way
At ease letting feelings out
Emotionally balanced individuals
Never hampered by self-doubt

Perfectly nurtured people
I wish I'd been the same
But something went wrong in childhood
No fingers, no pointing, no blame

Hovering on the outskirts
On the borderline of connection
Angst-ridden and incomplete
Living with imperfection